Twayne's English Authors Series

Sylvia E. Bowman, *Editor*

INDIANA UNIVERSITY

Benedict Kiely

(TEAS 145)

Benedict Kiely

By GRACE ECKLEY

Drake University

Twayne Publishers, Inc.　::　New York

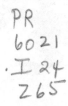

For Douglas, Stephen, Timothy

Preface

From a background of conflict described in *Counties of Contention*,[1] Benedict Kiely grew eventually to regard with pathos and humor the questions of politics and religion which have been blamed for dividing Ireland, a country in its totality measuring only thirty-two thousand square miles. In North Ireland, he grew up in a Nationalist and Catholic home where, two years after his birth, the British and Irish together determined that his native County Tyrone and five other Northern counties would be partitioned from the rest of Ireland and would remain a constituent part of the United Kingdom of Great Britain and Northern Ireland. As in the American Civil War, divisive and urgent questions of loyalties pitted family members and neighbors against one another and the problems continued into the 1940's when Kiely began writing and when Ireland's "false neutrality" during the war provoked renewed debate. In a letter to me in the spring of 1966, soon after the destruction of Dublin's famed Nelson Pillar, long a symbol of British domination, Kiely wrote, "The Nelson Pillar outrage is deplored by everybody with sense. But it's the sort of unfortunate thing that can still happen in Ireland. In a letter to *The Irish Times* I suggested that these half-educated poor devils would be better employed putting stink bombs in the office of the Censorship of Publications."[2] In his essay "Ulster After the Bludgeons" (*The Nation*, May 19, 1969), Kiely blames North Ireland's conservatives for the deplorable outrages begun once again in 1968; those activities extend rather than alleviate the ancient enmities.[3]

Naturally an Irish writer would hope that "stink bombs in the office of the Censorship of Publications" would accomplish more good than guerrilla warfare. Kiely has experienced such censorship (his novels *In a Harbour Green, There Was an Ancient House,* and *Honey Seems Bitter* were all banned, but the first two were later "unbanned" by the Appeals Board), but more recently he writes in his essay "The Whores on the Half-Doors" (1969) that some progress has been made in this other stronghold of conservatism: "In the 1940s when my own second novel [*In a Harbour Green*], a harmless piece, God knows, received the national literary award for being in general tendency indecent or obscene, the editor of a big Dublin daily, for which I then worked, told me, more in sorrow than in anger, that he couldn't give the book to his wife to read. In a better time and under more enlightened editorship the same paper came out strongly against the banning of John McGahern's *The Dark*." [4]

From North Ireland, after a year in a Jesuit seminary, Benedict Kiely moved to Dublin where his predilection for literature found a natural outlet, as well as earned Kiely a livelihood, in journalism. He began writing conventional Realistic novels on the themes he knew best: Nationalism and Catholicism in *Land Without Stars;* the propriety and provinciality of the small town in *In a Harbour Green;* disillusionment and loneliness in *Call for a Miracle* and *Honey Seems Bitter*. A new trend toward objectivity rather than conviction, and a reworking of folklore, began with *The Cards of the Gambler;* it concerns man walking, as Whitman phrased it, between the thought of death and the knowledge of death. The next novel, *There Was an Ancient House*, projects a seminarian's vacillation between faith and doubt about his worthiness for the high calling. *The Captain with the Whiskers* exposes the effect of one man's diabolism while casting serious doubt on his culpability; clearly the persons influenced by him were not totally deprived of freedom of choice. The recently completed novel, *Dogs Enjoy the Morning*, marks Kiely's greatest achievement in manipulating the Northern Ireland and Dublin settings to evoke humor and to perpetuate faith in nature, human and otherwise.

In writing this book, the first critical study of Kiely's work, I have attempted to prove that Kiely tells a good story well; to accomplish this, I have attempted to analyze his work both as art and as a means to achieving an understanding of Ireland and its people. Chapter 1, therefore, sets forth biographical details and opinions pertinent to Kiely's work. Chapter 2 summarizes Kiely's three nonfiction books—*Counties of Contention, Poor Scholar,* and *Modern Irish Fiction*—and some articles, especially the early writing which is not readily available in the United States but which establishes attitudes which continue into the very recent works.[5] Chapter 3 discusses plots and themes of the seventeen short stories in *Journey to the Seven Streams* and of ten other stories; and, thereafter to the conclusion, each chapter analyzes a separate novel in the order of publication. Chapter 12 attempts an overview of themes in all twelve books.

Acknowledgments

My deep appreciation for help in preparing this volume goes to Benedict Kiely, who graciously provided manuscripts and type-scripts, letters, and newspaper clippings, and further endeared himself by answering questions promptly and considerately; and to my husband, Wilton Eckley, for proposing the writing of this book.

Permissions to quote have been granted by Jonathan Cape of London, publishers of *In a Harbour Green* and *Call for a Miracle;* E. P. Dutton and Company of New York for American editions of *In a Harbour Green, Call for a Miracle,* and *Honey Seems Bitter;* The Mercier Press of Cork, Ireland, for *Counties of Contention;* Sheed and Ward of London and New York for *Poor Scholar;* Methuen of London for *Honey Seems Bitter, The Cards of the Gambler, There Was an Ancient House, The Captain with the Whiskers,* and *A Journey to the Seven Streams;* and Victor Gollancz of London for *Dogs Enjoy the Morning.*

For gratuitously providing out-of-print periodicals, the Irish "God bless" goes to J. J. Campbell of Belfast for copies of his *Irish Bookman* and to Father Henry of Dublin for typescripts and copies of *The Capuchin Annual.*

Contents

Chronology

1919   Benedict Kiely born August 15 in Dromore, County Tyrone, Ireland; father, Thomas Kiely; mother, Sarah A. Gormley.

1919   Moved to Omagh, County Tyrone.

1924   Attended Christian Brothers School at Omagh.

1936   Graduated from Christian Brothers School.

1936   Began contributions to Irish and English reviews.

1937   Entered Jesuit novitiate at Emo Paric, County Laois.

1938   Entered Cappagh Hospital, Finglas, Dublin.

1940   Matriculated at National University, Dublin.

1941   Began working for *The Standard,* a Dublin weekly, as feature writer and film critic.

1943   Awarded bachelor of arts degree in history, Latin, English.

1944   Married Maureen O'Connell.

1945   Daughter, Mary, born.

1945   *Counties of Contention* published by Mercier Press, Cork.

1946   Began work for daily paper, *The Irish Independent,* as member of editorial staff.

1946   First novel, *Land Without Stars,* published by Christopher Johnson, London.

1946   Daughter, Anne, born.

1947   *Poor Scholar, A Study of William Carleton (1794–1869)* published by Sheed and Ward, London and New York.

1949   Son, John, born.

1949   *In a Harbour Green* published by Cape, London, and E. P. Dutton, New York.

1950   *Modern Irish Fiction* published by Golden Eagle Books, Dublin.

1951   Began working for *Irish Press.*

1951   *Call for a Miracle* published by Cape, London, and E. P. Dutton, New York.

Chronology

1951 Daughter, Emer, born.
1952 *Honey Seems Bitter* published by Methuen, London and E. P. Dutton, New York.
1953 *The Cards of the Gambler* published by Methuen, London.
1955 *There Was an Ancient House* published by Methuen, London.
1960 *The Captain with the Whiskers* published by Methuen, London.
1961 *The Captain with the Whiskers* published by Criterion Books, New York.
1963 *A Journey to the Seven Streams, Seventeen Stories* published by Methuen, London.
1964 Came to the United States as writer-in-residence at Hollins College, Hollins College, Virginia.
1965 Served as visiting professor in creative writing, University of Oregon, Portland, Oregon.
1966 Served as writer-in-residence at Emory University, Atlanta, Georgia.
1968 Returned to Ireland.
1968 *Dogs Enjoy the Morning* published by Victor Gollancz, London.

CHAPTER 1

Amid Church Bells and Bugles:
Life and Literary Influences

I *Of Home and Family*

"ABOUT as big as a Jameson bottle," replied Benedict Kiely when asked how old he was when his family moved from his birthplace, Dromore, to Omagh in County Tyrone, North Ireland. There, Kiely grew up with a brother Gerald and three sisters: Rita, who married Thomas Connelly and lives in Dublin; Elieen, now Mrs. Frank McCrory of Belfast; and Kathleen, now Mrs. Brian Coll of Clarimore, North Ireland, whose home is the base for the Rafferty farm of *In a Harbour Green*.[1] A cousin, Joe Gormley, was the first person Kiely knew who spoke of the Tennessee Valley Authority; and, contrary to the outcome of *In a Harbour Green*, Joe succeeded in having the river valley drained. Kiely's paternal grandfather was a sergeant in the Royal Irish Constabulary and his father, who partly inspired the fictional fathers of several of Kiely's stories, was for some time in the Leinster regiment, garrisoned in Longford town, later sent to the Barbadoes in Jamaica. The Boer War in South Africa aborted the father's plans with a Munster friend to "jump" the army and to join the gold rush in the Klondike. He claimed to have met the famous General De Wet when De Wet was a prisoner of the Boers after the war.

In eastern North Ireland where the rivers Camowen and Drumragh meet to form the river Strule, Omagh presents all the features of union and disunion, of disinterest and enthusiasm common to Ireland's divided people. The novel *The Captain with the Whiskers* contains a description of such a city: "It was a religious little city just as Ireland is a religious little country. Those hilly streets ascended always to steeples and bells, and most of us climbed up to pray whether we meant it or not. But, being a seaport and a garrison town, it had for centuries its proud tradition of depravity, and reckless soldiers and sailors sought fun, and fought, in the pubs of the Fountain Lane gridiron under one corner of the walls, where even the white-putteed shore police, by gentlemanly agreement, left them to their recreations." [2]

The contrasts within a garrison town, such as Omagh, where the quartered British army, promising the glamor of India and Egypt, lured young men to disillusionment, gleam from the backgrounds of some of Kiely's work, especially in the humorous short story entitled "Soldier, Red Soldier," [3] and in the nostalgic novel *In a Harbour Green*.[4] Although the novel leaves a strong impression of concern for propriety on the part of the townspeople, the British army and "a lot of loose women," [5] as Kiely commented, made Omagh less proper than the average country town. There is in Ireland an old maxim that one never marries a girl from a garrison town because they were always reputed to be "half whores." In "Long After O'Neill," Kiely has written somewhat critically of Omagh:

There was a monastery once on a hill above the river Strule and tradition tells that a holy monk, in a moment of extreme melancholy, prophesied that the house of prayer would one day be a den of thieves. Later there was a jail in the same place, later still a military barracks; and the interpretation of the prophecy is still any man's game. Around the three of them, monastery, jail, barracks, the town of Omagh grew up and the effect of the three institutions on the character of the inhabitants is still clearly noticeable. . . . Over the old humpy bridge at Cregnagh, a portion of the Jacobite army must have passed going to and coming from the game of patience at Derry [an attempted blockade of the city, December 18, 1688 to July 28, 1689]. They still call it *The King's Bridge*. Then the town was burned two or three times, by accident or design. There was an Orange riot; Mitchel [John Mitchel, author of *Jail Journal* (1875)] mentions it. A murderer was hanged in the jail. A prisoner escaped from the same jail and a song was written about him, and to this day stories are told about his adventures and his great run before the black police [the "Black and Tans," a portion of the British Army]. And in quite recent days the town wards were gerrymandered to make straight the path of hegemony in local elections.[6]

Despite their opposed religious loyalties (Catholic versus Protestant), the people of this area during Kiely's memory of it generally existed on peaceful and friendly terms; he remembers a parish priest (though much of Irish history would indicate otherwise) who talked with Protestant and Catholic alike; [7] and yet the inhabitants of the area often feel the religious estrangement inherited from the past. Additional local color derives from a few native Gaelic speakers who were known in Kiely's youth in the Sperrin Mountains of the northwest; and, in some parts of the county, a Scotch burr was sometimes recognized in the accent. A unifying topic of continuing interest among all peoples, because the Irish of all places love sports, is the local Gaelic football competitions.

Omagh had, in addition in Kiely's time, a town poet [8] whose income came from various odd jobs and whose chief joy was "in writing the poor pieces of broken English that he called poems." Like others of the area, the poet was an admirer of Robert Burns, whose popularity Kiely explained in the *Capuchin* article; Burns was "the voice of a wild democracy that did almost unite Ireland." Though a Dryden-like satirist, this poet and others known and unknown have linked the ideals of the present with an idealized past, thereby contributing to Ireland's amazing volume of literature. The legends of this town and of its literature are, of course, the legends of all Ireland—of giant Cuchulain and strong Finn MacCool, of the tragic beauty of Deirdre and the golden beauty of Grainne, of Saint Patrick of nearby Armagh, and of the devoted Saint Colmcille. Politically, the activities of The Great O'Neill, who almost freed Ireland at the time of Queen Elizabeth, were also centered in this area.[9]

From this varied background with its own touches of distinction, including a poultry farm which sent white turkeys to the British royal table [10] and a man who indeed kept a cow in the house—[11] from the legends, the history, and the poets—are derived the reminiscences of a place which go into the making of a person. For Kiely himself, as he wrote of William Carleton, "the place has something symbolic of everything in the genius of the man that the place made." [12]

From attendance at the Christian Brothers School in Omagh, Kiely graduated to a Jesuit novitiate at Emo Paric [13] in County Laois, southwest of Dublin. After a year there he reported, as required by the order, an increasingly agonizing back ailment and promptly upon examination was removed to Cappagh Hospital at Finglas in County Dublin. His experiences as a novice are recorded in the novel *There Was an Ancient House,* and he has since commented that he now thinks he saw in the priesthood an opportunity to live an idealized life as a scholar. However, he abandoned the vocation during the eighteen months he spent in the hospital; and he has laughingly attributed his decision to do so to the irresistible attractions of young nurses.[14] During those months when he was forced to lie immobile while strapped to a back frame, reading and writing occupied nearly all his waking hours. In fact, since his efforts were aided by the Jesuits, who maintain excellent libraries, he read nearly everything available and acquired much of the "pedantry" which has appeared in subsequent novels and stories.

Once discharged from the hospital, without a job and without prospects, Kiely borrowed money from his brother and enrolled as a student at the National University, Dublin. A bachelor's degree was conferred in September, 1943, for studies in Latin, history, and English; and, although Kiely began a master of arts degree in history, he did not complete it, because by then he was fully launched in journalism.

As early as 1943, the "Long After O'Neill" article had appeared in *The Capuchin Annual;* and it was followed in the decade of the 1940's by more contributions to *The Capuchin Annual* and to the *Irish Bookman.* In 1945, his first book, *Counties of Contention,* was published; and, a year later, his first novel, *Land Without Stars,* appeared. In the mid-1950's he was elected to the Irish Academy of Letters.

Until the spring of 1964, Kiely's professional efforts were devoted to journalism and to the writing of articles, stories, and books. By 1960, the number of books totaled eleven. In 1964, Kiely visited the United States as a writer-in-residence at Hollins College, near Roanoke, Virginia. The next academic year, 1965–66, he was a visiting professor of creative writing at the University of Oregon; and, during the following two years, he held the same position at Emory University.

After coming to the United States, Kiely published a series of fortnightly articles in *The Irish Times.* Under the column title of "American Letters" or "Letters from America," they described the scenes and personalities he has observed and met, respectively, in his travels from coast to coast until his return to Ireland in

1968. Since then, his articles and short stories have continued to appear in various publications, and at the time of this writing he was preparing a book on Ireland as well as writing another novel.

Since 1968 the divisive personalities and situations of North Ireland have again claimed worldwide attention, and each "son of the soil" is frequently called upon to offer his interpretation of events there. Following a tour of his home land, Kiely wrote a succinct evaluation in October, 1969: "Diehard Unionism has, indeed, tried to save itself once again by using religious bigotry, but this time the game is up and something quite new has happened. The people most to be pitied are the ignorant Orangemen, urban and rural, who have for so long been *used* by their leaders, who still think the year is 1641 [the Ulster Rising against the British], and who are bewildered—but also dangerous." [15] The Irish tendency to look backward, rather than forward, keeps alive many memories of bravery against oppression but obviously deters much progress.

II   *Of Authors and Authorship*

Kiely shares his County Tyrone origins with William Carleton, the greatest Irish novelist of the nineteenth century, though Kiely, like Carleton, went on to Dublin, and, unlike Carleton, from there to America. With both literary and biographical pertinence, Kiely seconds the opinion of Carleton that William Butler Yeats expressed in the introduction to Carleton's *Irish Tales:* Carleton is "the greatest novelist of Ireland by right of the most Celtic eyes that ever gazed from under the brow of story-teller." [16] Kiely once said that Carleton better than any other Irish writer has recorded the personality of the Irishman and provided the key to the Irish heart, and Kiely cited the example of Carleton's Paddy-Go-Easy in *Parra Sastha* (1845).[17] Indeed, the matter of flood control in Kiely's *In a Harbour Green,* where an effort for improvement meets only frustration, occasions a rueful comment from Pat Rafferty: "My old man says that like Paddy-Go-Easy we're content with whatever contented our fathers." [18] With proper care, however, Paddy's land later becomes a model farm.

Among other writers who are Kiely's favorites are William Butler Yeats and James Joyce and, from the Classics, *The Golden Ass* of Lucius Apuleius. Quotations from Yeats, in particular, appear without quotation marks in Kiely's works as a part of the Irish scene in statements such as "The woodland paths are dry," or, in an "American Letter," "In the Heart of Old New England" (1966), Kiely recalls President Kennedy with the quotation, "Soldier, scholar, horseman, he,/ And all he did done perfectly,/ . . . What made us dream that he could comb grey hair?" [19]

When Kiely was asked what reading he early preferred, Kiely replied that his childhood reading was a "mixed bag." He remembers hearing Jonathan Swift's *Gulliver's Travels* and Sir Walter Scott's *Talisman* read aloud by his sister. In childhood also he enjoyed the detective thrillers of Edgar Wallace and the cowboy stories of Charles Alden Selster and Zane Grey. While in grade school, he first read Herman Melville's *Moby Dick* with "complete and teetotal incomprehension," a confusion later increased by John Barrymore's performance in the motion picture *The Sea Beast*, in which the altered story provides Ahab the solace of a woman and a happy ending. At home, he read much of G. K. Chesterton and Hilaire Belloc; at college, he popularized Graham Greene. "It's just a question of reading for the sake of reading," he said; but his loyalty to authorship goes beyond mere enjoyment. When James Joyce died in 1941, Kiely led a protest parade against the Dublin newspapers which sought to avoid honoring Joyce by not acknowledging his death. Unfortunately, this kind of loyalty from an Irish countryman still is rare in Ireland, although efforts are being made to improve Ireland's attitude toward its most famous writers. Such an effort is a collection of essays entitled *A Bash in the Tunnel* (1970), edited by John Ryan of Dublin. In it, Thomas F. Staley, editor of the *James Joyce Quarterly*, praised the articles by John Jordan and Benedict Kiely. He remarks, "Both writers clearly evoke the feeling of what it was for a younger generation of Irish writers to discover Joyce and in so doing rediscover their world which had in turn been Joyce's. This experience I had not read of before, and it meant a great deal to read these two essays, for it established for the first time what I knew must really be in Ireland—a sense of continuity between Joyce and a younger generation of writers." [20]

To achieve that rare "sense of continuity" with the writers of the Irish Literary Renaissance, Kiely began, as did James Joyce and many others, with the writing of poetry. He now relates humorously that it was "stopped providentially at the age of sixteen," and he prefers to disregard the poetry later published. He adds, "It was terrible poetry. I was keeping a magazine which was filled with all sorts of dire poems. When I ran short of a rhyme, I remember, I filled it in with the nearest four letter word that came to mind, and this was discovered. In the family I was reared in, instead of there being a sermon about it, it caused the most infinite amusement. It was read out and the ingenuity of the rhymes greatly admired." [21] At the age of thirteen Kiely wrote a novel called *Rebels in Spats* about an elderly English gentleman and his gentleman's gentleman who came to Ireland and were converted to the cause of the Irish revolution. Since freedom from English domination has been a problem for seven centuries, a problem nominally solved in the South with the creation of the Irish Free State in 1921 but continued into the present—so the Nationalists maintain—in North Ireland, Kiely chose his topic with appropriate nationalistic fervor. "I'm sure it was diabolical but my brother snitched the manuscript and has it hidden somewhere," said Kiely. "He won't surrender it and says ironically it's the best thing I ever wrote."

A first article submitted to a newspaper acquainted Kiely with the dismay of typographical errors. When Thomas Thoman, one of his three youthful friends who were known to him by their alliterative initials—F. F. (Frank Fox), L. L. L. (Lawrence Lee O'Laughlin), and T. T.—died of peritonitis, Kiely wrote about the funeral for the *Ulster Herald;* he substituted for the priest's sermon a more flowery one of his own composition. "I said 'the guerdon of something or other will be his,'" said Kiely, "and it was misprinted *querdon.*"

Kiely's professional writing began in Dublin in the 1940's with articles for *The Capuchin Annual,* and Kiely speaks with reverence of its extraordinarily capable editor, Father Senan. [22] "In his office," said Kiely, "I met and made friends with John Count McCormack, Jack Butler Yeats, and Maud Gonne—[23] all in one week." For a beginner, the fees for bits of poetry and essays which he contributed were impressive; "If you sold something to Father Senan, it was big money then," he said.

After Kiely read a paper on G. K. Chesterton to the Literary Society of University College, Dublin (the paper was later published in the *Irish Ecclesiastical Record*),[24] he was offered a job by Peter O'Curry, editor of the weekly newspaper *The Standard.*

At this time, Kiely had attempted another novel called *The King's Shilling* and had offered it to Dublin's Talbot Press; but its reader replied that his employers thought one could not make a hero of a deserter running from his duty. Peter O'Curry introduced Kiely to novelist Francis MacManus,[25] who was writing at that time a column for *The Standard* under the name of Manus Neil. Francis MacManus, soon becoming a good friend, read the novel, and said it would make an excellent long short story of eighteen thousand words. Annoyed and disappointed at the time, Kiely later agreed with MacManus and discarded huge portions of it. Subsequently, as Kiely's first long fiction, but still a short story, it was printed by J. J. Campbell in the *Irish Bookman*.

Anecdotes of Irish writers enliven both Kiely's published works and his conversations, partly because, since 1940, he has been in newspaper work where meeting people is a necessary part of the business. But also, he explains, Dublin is not so much a small city as an intimate city; and the much-touted social life of the Irish bars is important for contacts more than for drinking. But he failed to appreciate the unique social qualities of the pubs until he journeyed to London and America. "Outside Fleet Street, London," he said, "I've never found the good talk anywhere else." To his amusement, one American student said, "If you know all these people, what are you doing here?" As Kiely wrote in *Call for a Miracle*, "In Dublin everybody meets everybody."

III *Of Art and Art Theory*

Kiely's favorite technique of writing bits of dialogue, character sketches, and settings, and of then arranging them in novel sequence, may account in part for the effect of fragmentation found in his early writing—a problem that is overcome in the more closely unifed recent writing. One anecdote of his college teaching days reports his being surprised by a student when he was at work on his hands and knees on the floor surrounded by bits of paper covering the floors of two rooms.[26] Kiely sees a major problem of writing in the matter of making characters move in such logical sequence, a technique for which the theatrical term "blocking" provides a convenient label. He often tells the experience of a friend who was writing a novel, who set a character in a cornfield and then spent several weeks trying to write him out of it. To Kiely, "Anyone can write the high spots [intensely dramatic scenes] but not everyone can make a character walk up steps [or out of cornfields] sensibly." [27] After establishing sequence, he then rewrites the novel several times.

In his teaching creative writing to college students, he has refused to assign subjects because he believes that materials for writing are everywhere. In a corresponding view, when asked about the formation of his theory of art, Kiely replied that he has never attempted to formulate such. "Writing is a form of living," he said:

That's why I'm against textbooks on the types of the short story, which I think are false and wrong. Every short story or every anecdote that comes to you is a new living person and has to be treated as such, and it *is* a different experience. You'll even find students who tell you they have an idea for a story and ask what technique they should use. The only thing I can think of saying to them is just start writing it down. Write bits of it here and bits of it there. Write them in notebooks and on scraps of paper and shuffle them about and then try to see what you have written down. You'll find that your idea will create the technique that is necessary to express it.

I think the anthologies on types of the short story are doing harm to young people because they begin to think "What type of short story should I write?" I'll admit that Jung wrote about psychological types and that there are psychological types in people, but when you're meeting a new person you don't think "What psychological type is this person going to be?" You accept this person as a new person; and at the same time you accept any experience that will go into a piece of fiction or a novel and to some extent—I'm sure—into lyric poetry. It's a new living experience and has to be treated as such.

Now Joyce did formulate his own particular aesthetic theory in *The Portrait of the Artist* but I really doubt that his work developed much from it. I know that it is sometimes necessary to formulate an aesthetic theory, and it can be frequently very necessary for aestheticians, but I think in the actual practical business of writing, it's the fact that everything must be living—that this is a living experience. A writer has a living experience and tries to communicate it to other people as best he can. And that's the only theory of art you can have.[28]

CHAPTER 2

Toward Firbolgs and Moles:
The Nonfiction

W HEN the Act of Partition was signed in December, 1921,[1]
Benedict Kiely was only two years old; he was growing up
in a strongly Nationalist and Catholic family and living in one
of the six Unionist and predominantly Protestant counties of the
North which, by the Act of Partition, was separated from the
twenty-six remaining counties of Ireland. Geographically, his
family represented the losing side, and Kiely's early books of
nonfiction reflect the pathos of the Northerners who still desire
the nationality which the Southerners achieved. The problem
became more acute for a person maturing in the turbulent 1940's
when Ireland's "false neutrality" during World War II forced
attention to questions of loyalty. "It was something you had to
write out of your system," he explained. Of the two influences—
Nationalism and Catholicism—the Nationalism was "written out"
in his first book, *Counties of Contention* (1945) and in his first
novel, *Land Without Stars* (1946). At the time of writing, he had
crossed the border into Nationalist Dublin, from which he could
look back with increasing detachment to the opinions of North
Ireland—with so much detachment, in fact, that he has now
reversed his opinion (in spite of renewed violence in the late
1960's) and thinks the partition should remain. The other attachment of his youth, the Jesuit priesthood, still merits his warm
devotion so that novels such as the most recent one, *Dogs Enjoy
the Morning* (1968), though making religious literature a source
of humor, reveal a continuing sympathy.

Kiely's earliest writing derives from the social environment and
from the natural geography of the home area. Two articles,
"Journey in Ulster" and "Long After O'Neill," both published in
1943 in *The Capuchin Annual*, are travelogues of the nine coun-

ties of the North and of County Tyrone, respectively. At this time, the formalities of border regulations hurt deeply; they led Kiely, with thoughts of the great O'Neill, to comment in "Long After O'Neill" on the Strabane River as the "natural border between two counties that still, in spite of the folly of a score of years, are part of the same country; because the natural arrangement of things has an ancient validity that still outlasts huts of wood or concrete built to house revenue officers." Combining travelogue with biography and criticism, Kiely wrote in "Man from the Pampas" (1948, *The Capuchin Annual*) about William Bulfin, author of *Rambles in Eirinn*, first published in 1907; in his article Kiely formulates a theory which he applies to his own travel articles: "The book [Bulfin's] switches from the present to the past and from pleasantry to anger as all good travel-books should, for the journey has nothing that has not variety, and the good traveller goes as much through the past as through the present, and as bravely in the rain as in the sunshine." [2]

In this manner, from Donegal in the North ("A Present from Donegal," 1944), to Kerry in the South ("Land Without Stars," 1945–46), and an article on the great Daniel O'Connell entitled "The House at Derrynane" (1946),[3] Kiely selected materials first published in *The Capuchin Annual* and in the *Irish Bookman;* he has expanded or combined them with other articles to form the early books of nonfiction. The article entitled "Poor Scholar" first appeared in 1946 in the *Irish Bookman* [4] and then later provides the framework of the book, *The Poor Scholar, A Study of the Works and Days of William Carleton (1794–1869).*

I To Honor a Countryman

Among Kiely's three books of nonfiction, the second, *Poor Scholar,* holds first place in chronological order; it gives the background of the nineteenth-century experiences of the Irish people which best explain the violent and confused emotions of the early twentieth century. Those emotions which were generated by the arbitrary partition of the country in 1921 is the subject of the first book of nonfiction, *Counties of Contention;* the literary trends, many of which were inspired by the national rivalries of the period 1890–1930, became the subject of Kiely's third book of nonfiction, *Modern Irish Fiction (1930–1950).*

The term "poor scholar," in its strictest sense, designated an

Irish youth who traveled to Maynooth, the center of instruction for the priesthood, and sustained himself while there by giving lessons in various homes which could provide food and shelter for as little as one night or as long as possible. Carleton once began such a journey, and, though he soon returned home, deserves such an epithet as Kiely applied to him because, in another sense, his schooling was of the poor "hedgeschool" variety. Where formal schooling was for a time under British domination almost un-known, learning survived somewhat precariously through the agency of hedgeschool masters, a strange breed of itinerant pedants whose scholarly qualifications were likely to be as ill-assorted as their methods of teaching, and often the subjects they taught, were unorthodox. Assembled under the uncertain Irish skies, in the ditch, along the side of the road, the hedgeschool was appropriately named. There tattered, hungry, and shivering children stretched their usually bare toes toward a small turf fire and learned to read and write by sketching letters on the ground with a stick. These scenes, which Carleton describes vividly in his novels, Kiely in turn evokes in his book on Carleton.

One of the most poignant passages of Kiely's biography de-scribes a scene Carleton witnessed in County Louth. Under road-side gallows lounged a few British soldiers who were officially guarding a high-swinging tar sack containing the body of one Paddy Devaun. The pitch aided the putrefaction of flesh, which oozed to the ground in streams of slime. Carleton listened to the story of Paddy Devaun, who had opposed evictions of the Irish by English soldiers, and subsequently he observed altogether twenty-four such bodies in that district. In another passage, Kiely quotes Carleton's description of famine as Carleton recorded it in *The Black Baronet:* "Famine meant twenty-three human beings, of all ages and sexes, as the public officers said, lying together on the same straw-littered floor, five or six of them already putrid corpses. . . . Mothers tottered off under the woeful excitement of misery and frenzy, and threw their wretched children on the side of the highways, leaving them there, with shouts of mirth and satisfaction, to perish or be saved . . . whilst fathers have been known to make a wolfish meal upon the dead bodies of their own offspring." [5]

Among the varied methods available for writers of biography,

Kiely chose to write his biography of Carleton mainly from his knowledge of William Carleton's works as they revealed his experiences. In such accounts of Carleton's activities or thoughts, where the supposition reasonably extends from the recognized source, the words "possibly" or "maybe" are frequently inserted to mark scrupulously the exact position of departure from the verified fact. A valuable source of fact is Carleton's autobiography, the last book he wrote and which he left unfinished (his contemporary David J. O'Donoghue edited it and published it in 1896).[6] Into the narrative drawn from these sources, Kiely inserted excerpts from Carleton's stories, thereby giving a dramatic and realistic touch. Such excerpts usually contain the dialect speech which Carleton wrote for his characters.

Another part of Kiely's technique is to place Carleton among his contemporaries—Maria Edgeworth, Daniel O'Connell, Charles Lever, Thomas Davis—[7] and to discuss Carleton's views along with the writing, deeds, and opinions of these other persons. At times, this method of writing biography permits the inclusion of adverse criticism, as in Kiely's comment on Carleton's statement that Gerald Griffin, John Banim,[8] and William Carleton were the only three great Irish writers. Kiely says: "No one could with justice accuse him of unreasoning vanity; but the sweeping nature of that statement might raise doubts as to whether he had the balance or the equipment necessary for a survey of the origin, development, decline and revival of Irish literature" (179).

In *Poor Scholar,* Kiely preserves the varying moods of Carleton, who changed his religion and politics as circumstances varied. As for Carleton's contradictory writing on both sides of several issues, Kiely thinks his vacillation may have derived from Carleton's peasant background, which would naturally seek defense "against the superiority of people born in high houses." And Kiely adds that such a complex also "evidenced itself in an effort to interpret ways of life about which he knew little or nothing." That he led a varied life among many kinds of people in Ireland, however, and was able to convey naturalistic details in colorful, moving stories explains why today Carleton's books remain essential for understanding the backgrounds and the attitudes in the works of such major Irish authors as Yeats and Joyce. Kiely concludes, "His importance is that he gave life without end to a vanishing, perishing people, saw something in their souls, and in the outward manifestation of their spirit that joins them solidly across the centuries to the people of this present time" (124).

With careful exposure of both merits and faults of this County Tyrone predecessor whom he much admires, Kieiy's book on Carleton is more objective than *Counties of Contention*. This, his first book, reveals the intense Nationalism of Kiely's youth.

II *To Right a Wrong*

In *Counties of Contention*, Kiely attempts to explain the religious and political misunderstandings which resulted in the 1921 division of Ireland. In doing so, he lays the blame heavily upon Edward Carson, a North Ireland Protestant; seeks to show that a sizable Catholic population should be exonerated of responsibility for such division; and assumes that a united Ireland is the desire and goal of both the Northern and the Republic of Ireland citizens of 1945.

Central to the misunderstandings dividing a small country is confusion about the terms intended to identify the conflict. Such terms most frequently used and misused are "Unionist," "Nationalist," and "Ulster." The "Unionists," as Kiely explains, "stood for the union of Ireland and England under one crown, one legislature, one administration." [9] A Nationalist desired free and independent government for Ireland. Ulster, in the opening years of the twentieth century, meant an area comprising nine counties roughly approximating the old historic province of Ulster in the northeast portion of the island around the city of Belfast. Here, compared with the remaining three provinces, the proportion of Protestants to Catholics was substantially larger, dating from the time of King James I of England who in the early seventeenth century had introduced a number of Calvinist planters from Scotland. But the term "Ulster," in its present loose and inaccurate usage, derives from the debate about the Third Home Rule Bill at the time of the beginning of World War I, and it identifies the six counties of Armagh, Derry, Fermanagh, Tyrone, Antrim, and Down which now constitute North Ireland.

The question of how any people, especially of the twentieth century, could desire any other than independent government poses some mean problems in what the poet William Butler Yeats would have called the use of "politic words." [10] According to Kiely, the preference for union with Britain originated in the mind of a young and powerfully rhetorical lawyer, Edward Carson, to whom the term electorate meant "the united voters of England, Ireland, Scotland, and Wales, joined in one kingdom under one crown" (21). "For the majority of Irishmen," Kiely adds, "it meant only the people of Ireland possessed of the power to decide their own national destiny, ready to live amicably with England only when that power was recognised" (21). To stress these two divergent viewpoints of Carson and of the majority, Kiely lists the evils that Carson believed would result from independent government:

the old civil service would disappear; the protective police would be taken away; religious education would be in the hands of the Nationalist Party and that meant compulsory Papistry and compulsory Gaelic; there could be no appeal except to a Parliament in College Green. Then the Unionist minority would gain nothing by Home Rule. "Do you gain financial advantage by dissolving partnership with the Exchequer of the richest country in the world? [said Carson]. Do you gain greater civil freedom in abandoning a government which has been an example of liberty to every foreign nation? Do you gain greater religious freedom?" (23)

With the vociferous Carson pointing the dangers of independence and achieving recognition as the typical Ulsterman, Home Rule to the Protestant proletariat of the North came to mean "the Pope, the scarlet woman, the Papishes riding in triumph, King William and the Boyne only memories, the drum silenced, the crown of England in the dust, the citadel betrayed" (49) as well as industrial slump and unemployment. In resistance to a Home Rule Bill, the Carsonites formed an army called the Ulster Volunteer Force; and, in anticipation of a visit by Sir Winston Churchill, who favored Home Rule, they drilled, marched, and climactically snubbed him with the riotous closing of the doors of Ulster Hall. In the South, the Irish Volunteers, without the freedom to transport arms, smuggled guns into Howth. Of Carson's responsibilities in this counteraction, Kiely comments, "Edward Carson was not by any means responsible for the ideals that sent Pearse, Clarke, Plunkett, MacDonagh to quicklime graves; but all the drilling volunteering and gun-running of his followers made it easier for Nationalist Ireland to think that its problems could be solved only with the gun" (53).

Another of those confusing terms is "Orangeism," a term which, like Ulster, signifies support of the British but particularly stresses loyalty to William of Orange and Protestantism. The Orange Society was organized in 1795 as a secret society for whose special garments, symbols, signs, passwords Kiely imputes a Freemasonry connection. Orangemen tended to disregard oppressive land tenures and independent spirit as causes of the current Irish disorder; rather, they blamed Rome, referring to "the imp of exclusive salvation . . . the profligate Church, the Mother of Harlots, whose religion is the paganism of the Caesars, dressed in the cerements of the Man of Calvary" (67). Regardless of these conflicting passions, however, 1917 statistics show enrolled in the Nationalist Volunteer Force, under the leadership of the Northern Irish parliamentarian John Redmond, 94,000 Catholics and only 64,000 Protestants fighting for Britain (90).

By 1914 several plans for partition had been proposed, along with federation and parliamentation of, perhaps, Scotland, Wales, London, the English Midlands, Yorkshire, and Lancashire as possible alternatives to both Home Rule and Irish independence. The Ulster Protestants, however, still feared discrimination against them under Home Rule; and various proposals from both sides now suggested time limits of three, six, or ten years for exclusion of four, six, or nine counties from Home Rule. After 1916, Britain's Lloyd George made himself unpopular by writing to Edward Carson that "We must make it clear that at the end of the provisional period Ulster does not, whether she wills it or not, merge in the rest of Ireland" (142).[11] The Ulster Unionist Council was strongest in six counties; isolation of all nine counties would have meant that, with county option, enough Nationalists would have been included to vote the area back into a united Ireland—or, at least, the Unionists seemed to analyze the political situation in this manner and, accordingly, to estimate their strength. Then, writes Kiely, with Lloyd George leaning strongly toward the Unionists and seeing their portion of Ireland distinctly separate from the other, without granting county option, the Government of Ireland Act of 1920, known as the Partition Act, became law. It was called a mockery of the sacrifices of those who had died for Irish independence; the "clean cut" separation of six counties left hurt, anger, and frustration to explode in acts of slander, criminality, and injustice even to the present. Kiely's view of the Partition Act, when he wrote this book in 1945, was summarized in the succinct sentence that "it made no peace."

King George V of England came to Belfast City Hall to open its first parliament and declared his confidence in fairness to every faith, thus repeating a need for protection of religious minorities already outlined in the Partition Act. As late as the anonymous publication of the documented "Orange Terror" in 1943 (written by J. J. Campbell), Catholics of Northern Ireland could, however, expect victimization; or, as Kiely puts it, a Catholic's "house may be raided, he may be stopped and searched on the street, he may without accusation, trial or sentence be interned for indefinite periods" (173). Subsequent speeches by such persons as Sir Winston Churchill tended to gloss over the scars left by the Partition and to prove a nonexistent accord within the divided legislature. The last chapter of *Counties of Contention* is an analysis of "Orange Terror," a symposium of essays published in the 1943 *Capuchin Annual.*

Though Kiely at present disagrees with the views he expressed in 1945, *Counties of Contention* remains a worthwhile study of the attitudes of a large number of people and of some of the events in the period 1900–40. Of enduring interest, also, for appreciators of Irish literature are the passages about Maud Gonne and William Butler Yeats. Of Maud Gonne, Kiely wrote that the poor people of Mayo and the Rosses of Donegal "saw her almost as the reincarnation of some beauty of Gaelic legend," and that "led by a generous, impulsive heart [she] became a legend to the grateful poor, and drew his greatest poems from the greatest poet [William Butler Yeats] of his time" (29).

Of the relationship of the emerging Irish literature of the time to the political situation, though its best was branded "damned rebellious rant" when recognized at all by Unionist Belfast, Kiely writes a beautiful tribute, especially to Yeats: "he was a poet, not a politician; he was sternly, even arrogantly consistent to the ideal fascination of what's beautiful; and when he was stirred to write that remarkable salutation to terrible beauty [the poem, "Easter 1916"] he found that beauty, not in the speeches of Edward Carson, but in the gallantry of the young men who defied a great Empire, because they genuinely believed and were ready to die for those beliefs" (109).

Kiely, continuing his appreciation of the Irish scene, wrote in the years 1946–48 for the *Irish Bookman* a series of articles from which much of the book *Modern Irish Fiction* was to develop. These articles have the following subjects: James Stephens in "Clay and Gods and Men"; Francis Sylvester Mahoney (Father Prout) in " 'So Grand On . . .' " (1946); Liam O'Flaherty in " 'Connachtman's Grumbles' "; Shan F. Bullock in "Orange Lily"; Jane Barlow in "Yesterday Is Forever" (1947); Daniel Corkery in "Chronicle by Rushlight"; and Sean O Faolain in "Marooned Modernist?" (1948).[12]

III *To Survey an Epoch*

In *Modern Irish Fiction, A Critique,* Kiely has attempted the momentous task of drawing conclusions about Irish literature in the period 1930–50 from a catalogue of approximately fifty Irish writers, and in the Postscript he acknowledges omissions. Beginning with the recognition of the suspicion that "the men without a struggle are the men without a story"—a criticism frequently leveled at Irish writers since the achievement of independence—Kiely proceeds on his own reiterated assumption that "in the whole chronicle of man on earth no story has ever been told to the end." [13] The similarities of those chronicles, however, as they appear in the works of those fifty writers, make possible a reduction—at least for purposes of convenience—to eight topics or chapters: rebels, peasants, townsmen, heroes, history, dreams, exiles, lovers and creeds.

As Kiely views the topic "rebels," it is to Daniel Corkery, chiefly in *The Threshold of Quiet* and *The Hounds of Banba,* that one may turn for stories of contemplatives in revolution, quiet men who accept their people but rebel against unnecessary restriction. Corkery's revolution, based on his preference for Henry David Thoreau, must be one in the soul. Turning from Corkery's acceptance of his people and their hopes, one sees the alternative rejection by the young James Joyce, reaching his *non serviam* doctrine; and, in contrast, one has the excitement of Frank O'Connor's stories in *Guests of the Nation,* in which the characters seem to enjoy revolution. Brinsley MacNamara in *The Clanking of Chains* offers yet another view, one of disillusionment, "the fad-

ing out of the Yeatsian red flare of dreams." Still another view—
that of Liam O'Flaherty in *The Informers, The Assassin,* and
Mr. Gilhooley—reveals the possibilities revolution provides for
drawing great gestures from degraded men; and Sean O Faolain
in *Come Back to Erin* presents the character of Frankie Hannafey,
a revolutionary without a revolution, who becomes an exile in the
city of Cork.

Greater consistency in attitudes can be found, Kiely thinks,
among peasants than among rebels, perhaps because the relationship to the land is a primary consideration from which government, as Rousseau would have it, secondarily develops, and
because the instincts of land ownership belong to people in
general. Seamus O'Kelly in *Wet Clay* jestingly defines the peasant
in the words of a farmer: "Our instinct was always aristocratic.
We only allowed that we were peasants when we were noble,
bold, or better still, proprietors." An exaggerated sense of ownership grips the souls of Francis MacManus' novel *This House Was
Mine;* and his trilogy—*Stand and Give Challenge, Candle for
the Proud,* and *Men Withering*—about the Gaelic poet Donnacha
Rua MacConmara deals with the land hunger of the dispossessed.
Liam O'Flaherty in *The Black Soul* tells of a war-scarred man
returning to Inverara to find peace. Shan F. Bullock in *The Lough-
siders* presents the prosperous Northern Protestant farmer; and
Michael McLaverty, also writing about Ulster near Belfast in *Call
My Brother Black, Lost Fields,* and *In This Thy Day,* contrasts
the desirability of the lovely rural Ireland with the ugliness of
industrial black Belfast where a quality of innocence acquired
through remembered green fields and clear skies continues to
characterize displaced rural people who must deal with city
poverty and politics. Another side of peasant nature, crusted with
cow dung and thwarted by cunning relatives and preachers, is
comically caricatured in Patrick Kavanagh's novel *Tarry Flynn.*

In the chapter entitled "Townsmen," Kiely describes Irish writing about town life as centered in the three cities of Dublin, Cork,
and Belfast. James Joyce, said Kiely, was "the first Irish writer
to feel about the streets as Carleton and others had felt about
the fields, as Maria Edgeworth and others had felt about the
big house of the landed gentry" (45). Other writers—Kate O'Brien,
Brinsley MacNamara, Kenneth Reddin, and J. H. Pollock—mention Dublin; but Joyce was the first Irish writer "to see the corpo-

rate life of a city or a town as something with a universal meaning" (46). Frank O'Connor, Sean O Faolain, and Daniel Corkery write about their native Cork City. Forrest Reid in his novel *Peter Waring* and in his autobiography *Apostate* and Michael McLaverty in *Call My Brother Black* write about Belfast.

A survey of heroes in Irish literature of this period brings from Kiely some of his best criticism. Beginning with the nineteenth-century, Standish O'Grady, who "brought the heroes into Irish literature" and imparted dignity to giants who talked with Saint Patrick in *Finn and His Companions*, the stories of Irish heroes invariably reach into the past when men were demigods and when a mixture of the strange and real was accepted without question. Yeats wrote of "personal emotion woven into a general pattern of myth and symbol," and this treatment characterizes James Stephens' *Deirdre*, the same Stephens who also in *The Crock of Gold* wrote of leprechauns attacking a policeman and in *The Demigods* of an angel coming down to earth to mingle with a tinker's daughter. Austin Clarke, whom Kiely calls "the best living Irish poet," put together in one book, *The Singing Men at Cashel*, "dreams and visions, the adventures of Anier the poet, the loves of Gormlai, the ascetic life and violent death of Cormac" (68). In Eimar O'Duffy's *King Goshawk and the Birds*, Cuchulain returns with a Shavian desire to fight the evils of capitalism; and in Flann O'Brien's *At Swim Two Birds*, Finn MacCool becomes, among drunken Dublin undergraduates, boisterously comic. Witchcraft and wizardry appear in Mervyn Wall's picaresque novels *The Unfortunate Fursey* and *The Return of Fursey*.

History as a theme for Irish literature in the 1930–50 period, as Kiely sees it, disperses Irish fictional creations among varied centuries and continents. Joseph O'Neill in *Wind from the North* journeys back to the tenth century and to the Norse city of Dyflin buried under the present Dublin. In *Land Under England* and *Day of Wrath*, O'Neill comes to what Kiely calls a disillusioned-Wellsian future; and in *Chosen by the Queen*, a novel about Essex, he masters the idiom of the past. Francis MacManus earns consideration here once more for the biography of Donnacha Rua MacConmara that is phrased in "sentences hard like bricks built around a tomb" (83). Sean O Faolain's past in *A Nest of Simple Folk* and in *Bird Alone* concerns the fathers and grandfathers of Irish revolutionaries in careful character studies which Kiely sees as "a comment on rather than a complete denial of the popular notion of the perfect patriot" (86). Kate O'Brien in *Without My Cloak* has chronicled the middle-class Considine family of the previous century, and in *That Lady* she has presented a case of conscience revolving on the story of Ana de Mendoza and Philip II of Spain. Liam O'Flaherty in *Famine,* which Kiely views as his best novel, deals with the temporary rise of Thomsy Hines from suffering in a peasant community to faintly realized hope while hearing talk of revolution. Philip Rooney in his *North Road* successfully describes the figure of Galloping O'Hanlon, and in his *The Golden Coast* a wanderer returns from piracy to contentment under the Dublin stars.

Dreams, or the problem of distinguishing the real from the unreal, varies from that which borders on insanity—as in Mary Lavin's *The Becker Wives* in which Flora strokes an imaginary green dragon—to the "concrete romanticism" of Francis Stuart. Between these extremes are Brinsley MacNamara's *The Valley of the Squinting Windows* and *The Various Lives of Marcus Igoe,* which Kiely considers MacNamara's best book. These novels of Brinsley MacNamara draw from Kiely a comment about the artistic importance of windows: "For the fantasist and the dreamer a window is supremely important. They can look out through it and see the world and still know that their detachment is preserved by a barrier that, even if it is transparent, can only be broken by a most inartistic violence" (95). Looking through a window in Forrest Reid's *Peter Waring* makes Peter feel that he is actually invisible, and such a person becomes aware of a world of his own. A man with a pictorial imagination, Jack B. Yeats, has written the three novels—*Sailing, Sailing Swiftly,* and *The Careless Flower*—in which characters "relive in pictures their more vital experiences." Francis Stuart wrote: "There is always more in life than meets the eye"; and, to incorporate the best of Romanticism and Realism, he wrote *The Angel of Pity, Try the Sky,* and *Pidgeon Irish* in a technique which he called "concrete romanticism," and which Kiely describes, acknowledging a Kafka influence, as having "spiritual intensity and a sort of anarchical meaning." And Kiely identifies Joyce's vast dream *Finnegans Wake* as the book that Giovanni Papini proposed to write but did not, and which was to be called "Adam" or "The Record of Mankind" and was to contain man's history in two thousand tersely written pages.

Joyce provides the bulk of material for the chapter entitled "Exiles," after which Kiely comments, "There is hardly an Irish writer who does not touch somewhere on the exile or the idea of exile"—perhaps merely because the country is a small one where it is "economically impossible to keep everybody at home." The self-imposed exile of Joyce is seen as the result of the environment's post-Parnell bitterness; but other persons vanished or returned for less dramatic, for economic, or for nostalgic reasons. Patrick MacGill in *The Black Bonar* details the horrors of the exiled Irish working in the Scots praty and cinder fields; Daniel Corkery in *Earth Out of Earth* tells of an exile's returning in his old age to hear, in person, Jack McCormack sing. Others writing of exile include Sean O Faolain. Kate O'Brien, Shan F. Bullock, Forrest Reid, Frank O'Connor, Elizabeth Bowen, Francis Stuart, and Francis MacManus.

The chapter entitled "Lovers and Creeds" bravely attempts two huge topics: religion and love. Religion in Daniel Corkery's *The Stormy Hills* is an acceptance of faith, and the work of James Joyce is a rejection of it, a necessary artistic defiance of the gods for freedom to create. Love is a theme in the work of Kate O'Brien, and religion and love in conflict is a theme in the work of several novelists. For Kiely, the topic of love induces discussion of Irish literary censorship, the codology of which is "matter for the humourist and . . . matter for the pathologist"; and the code draws from Kiely the indictment that "in general tendency indecent" invariably is applied to any work dealing with "love between man and woman." [14] Almost with glee Kiely points to Kate O'Brien's title *The Land of Spices* obviously destined for interpretation by some readers as "spicy" or sensational but actually extracted from a George Herbert sonnet which recurrently employs the word "prayer." Treating religion and love together, Kiely examines works of Sean O Faolain, Kate O'Brien, Frank O'Connor, Patrick MacGill, Francis MacManus, Francis Stuart, and Elizabeth Bowen.

A stylistic problem in *Modern Irish Fiction* apparently develops from a modest assumption that the reader is as well informed as the author; Kiely tends to introduce the main subject in a subordinate position and to name literary characters for comparisons without citing author or title of the work in which they appear. An important attraction is the appended bibliographical and biographical notes which are especially valuable because there are few sources which include this recent material.

IV *Other Nonfiction*

Upon his arrival in the United States in September, 1964, Kiely continued to write nonfiction in the form of fortnightly "American Letters" or "Letters from America" to *The Irish Times* in Dublin, numerous book reviews for the *New York Times* and periodicals, and essays for periodicals. In the "American Letters," Kiely returns to the travelogue format of some of the early *Capuchin* articles. With visual detail and idiomatic speech, he records the varied moods of America; he traveled in four years through more sections of the country than many well-traveled Americans see in their entire lives. In addition, he succeeds in obeying his own dictum about travel books, the one previously expressed about William Bulfin; he goes "as much through the past as through the present, and as bravely in the rain as in the sunshine."

The "American Letters" reveal that in Roanoke, Virginia, though the Irish generally oppose blatant commercialism, Kiely learned to admire the genial and gigantic Mr. Peanut sign; in Oregon, he observed and then wrote appreciably about Basque sheepherders who squirted wine from a goatskin pouch. In Salt Lake City, he not only toured Mormon buildings but also read *The Book of Mormon;* in the Midwest, he linked the Wabash with Theodore Dreiser; [15] in Reno, he compared statistics on marriage and divorce; in San Francisco, he found a John M. Synge play being performed in Chinatown; in New England, he remembered the Kennedy wedding party of 1953 when he viewed the home of Hugh D. Auchincloss in 1966. While witnessing a murder and reading of others, watching Americans act from their enthusiasms and their prejudices, going from the Playboy Club to a Negro church, conversing at length with the atheist Thomas Altizer,[16] showing in the story of Leo Frank how an anti-Jewish mob lynched an innocent man in 1913, listening to the North Ireland fundamentalist Ian Paisley speaking in a Baptist tabernacle in Georgia, Kiely still retained memories of the people at home. For the friends in Dublin, he ended one American letter humorously:

"Even Brothers Horgan and MacReamonn will have to admit
that there could be nothing more ecumenical than for an ex-Jesuit
from Omagh, Tyrone, to be saved in Marietta, Georgia, by a
Fundamentalist woman from Ballymena, Antrim." [17]

Kiely's nonfiction includes many book reviews and articles, and
these in recent years reveal his steadily expanding background for
comparisons. From distant America, after looking back on a lifetime in Ireland, Kiely wrote a summation of two types of Irishmen
in a review of the book *Joseph Holloway's Abbey Theatre* (edited
by Robert Hogan and Michael J. O'Neill) for the *Northwest
Review:* "My own native isle of the ocean has in the course of its
history produced two very odd peoples: the Firbolgs and the
Moles. . . . The Moles are backbiters, begrudgers, censors of
books, miraculous meddlers, members of the Total Abstinence
Association who go on parades to prove to the Sacred Heart, who
couldn't care less and who liked a drop himself, and to the
benighted world, that they, heroically, do not drink." [18] As one
of the Moles, Joseph Holloway himself inspires Kiely's satire. In
contrast, after the publication of John Barth's *Giles Goat-Boy*
(1966), Kiely wrote a review of Barth's works which permitted
ample display of Kiely's vast knowledge of literature and mythology. Kiely regards the aim of *Giles Goat-Boy,* an aim he praises
highly and realizes in some of his own fiction, "to swive life
steadily and swive it whole." [19]

To Kiely, the new nonfiction sometimes indicates alignments
of apparently disparate backgrounds and authors. In his essay,
"Green Island, Red South," Kiely compares some of the writers
of Ireland's North, particularly Mary Lavin, with those of America's South as described by Flannery O'Connor. A common point
of unity, no doubt, is the dominant Catholic content of writers
from the green island and the red South—red by virtue of its clay
soil. Disagreeing with Flannery O'Connor's opinion that the
"Catholic sacramental view of life is one that maintains and supports at every turn the vision that the storyteller must have if he
is going to write fiction of any depth," Kiely succinctly retorts,
from a past of contention in those matters, "in one country in the
world where the Catholic sacramental view of life has had its
way . . . it has created a climate hostile to literature and writers;
the Irish writer being regarded by the church and the churchgoers
as a cross (there's a pun there, if you want a pun) between the

village idiot and the socially irresponsible rake who runs away with his neighbour's wife." [20]

While these brief comments on Kiely's nonfiction reveal only a little of its range and variety, they are intended to indicate his three main concerns—Irish nationality, the Catholic faith, and literary criticism. Each of the three books—*Poor Scholar, Counties of Contention,* and *Modern Irish Fiction*—has a distinct atmosphere as each in turn evokes, first, the vivid pictures of life in nineteenth-century Ireland; second, the rhetorical bombast of political bigotry at the beginning of the twentieth century; and, third, sketches of the various interpretations of Irish life by other writers of the 1930–50 period. The short nonfiction draws from Kiely's backgrounds in Ireland, North Ireland, and America; with such varieties of experience in combination, it is as much literary as geographic, as much critical as descriptive.

CHAPTER 3

Rich and Rare Gems: The Short Fiction

S EAN McMahon, when he commented on Kiely's fiction for *Eire-Ireland,* described it as "glowing with eloquence and distinguished by a facility that makes writing seem as easy as singing. Indeed, if he has a fault, it is a tendency to be operatic. Some people have been disconcerted by this and by an occasional contrived brilliance when he is too consciously a performer. He has been accused of sentimentality, an odd fault in so realistic a writer." [1] But not merely Kiely's diction makes the prose work poetic or operatic; both his sentences and his paragraphs are rhythmically and symmetrically constructed, as is shown in the following paragraph, which begins simply, swells like a cresendo in its most descriptive long sentence at the center, and again falls away into simplicity:

Then somewhere in the crowd a student threw into the air a roll of toilet paper. As it went up it unwound to drape itself around a trolley cable. In two minutes the air was thick with soaring and unwinding and descending rolls of toilet paper, the street rustled like a beechwood, black Belfast roared with laughter at the indecorous scheme of municipal decoration. The trams moved with a heave and a great effort. The moving trolleys set the paper burning and falling. Andrew laughed along with Belfast. [2]

It is his ability to catch the spirit of the trivial as well as of the great which yields sentiment, in itself a somewhat necessary quality; and Kiely's stories indicate that he considers poetic prose a necessary quality of good writing.

Kiely frequently constructs his short stories, seventeen of which have been collected in the volume *A Journey to the Seven Streams,* on an episode recalled or on an idea illuminated by a bit of conversation. The stories are very colorful, and they are narrated with a humorous restraint which, perhaps, develops naturally from the Irish tendency of understatement. Frequently, understatement means that obvious connections are omitted, as in this example from "The White Wild Bronco":

> "He has good blood in him," Tansey said. "I'll try him in a trap."
> Some of the fragments of the trap, they say, were found fifty yards away. . . . (16)

Another stylistic device, the sentence fragment, also aids brevity and compression, but it appears most frequently in the earlier stories. At the beginning of a paragraph, it clarifies a situation and marks the passage of time. "A whole tortured fortnight," for example, appears as a sentence after a lapse of time indicated by a space to mark the accumulating doubts and unresting dismay of a woman in love. Individuality of style includes, also, a tendency to mix adjectives, prepositional phrases, and participles in sequence: "Edmund, of an age with myself, bright brown eyes darting upwards from under a low fringe of curly hair that would never lie back straight as he wanted it to do, did try to talk." [3]

In subject matter, Kiely draws the short stories mostly from his North Ireland background, and most frequently he uses the name of Ballyclogher for his fictional Omagh. Other names which reappear are Jack MacGowan for a theatrically inclined friend and Gormley, his mother's family name, for farm or quarry. He allows tales of military exploits to hover in the background, not because of revolution, but because of his father, as in "Wild Rover No More"; and he treats thematically the military life that he has known from residence in a garrison town. His love of poetry, especially of ballads, appears in several places when appropriate lines, usually without quotation marks and in prose rather than verse form, fill a paragraph. In all stories, sympathy, gentle humor, and understanding mark the Kiely treatment of all types of people. To appreciate his versatility, one should contrast the sentimental vignette "The Little Wrens and Robins" with the poignant, bawdy, humorous story "A Ball of Malt and Madame Butterfly."

I *By Captain's Commands*

The earliest of Kiely's short fiction, "The King's Shilling," [4] was first intended to demonstrate the loveliness of the Strule Valley in the hay-cutting season; by the time of its publication, however, Kiely had edited it carefully and had minimized details of setting to let plot and character predominate. In the narrative, the escape of young Mickey Given from the British army, where he had been lured by huge recruitment posters and where he had quickly experienced disillusionment and homesickness, catapults him into a series of adventures. While seeking shelter from both military and civilian police, he is torn between the North Ireland people's alternate sympathy and hostility. To take the king's shilling means to join the British army. In the end, the daughter of the returned American for whom he had worked places in the hand of a British captain a shilling for which she pretends to buy Mickey's freedom; the captain, newly aglow and magnanimous in his successful courting of the girl, helps Mickey across the border. Kiely has not made Mickey an antihero in the sense of a person who merely accepts rather than directs his fate. Though a deserter, Mickey quickly uses his fists and his heavy military boots to beat his adversaries' flesh into unsightly bruises and swellings; he risks his stolen freedom to win a bicycle race from the local policeman champion; and, except for loyalty to an Irish lass, at times he seems destined to win the love of the American's daughter.

The lure of far places also characterizes Awkward John, the milkman, in "Soldier, Red Soldier," [5] which is dedicated to Padraic Colum, "whose poem provided the title." The villain of the story, Sergeant Cooper, has cooperated with the schoolmasters to teach small boys the rigors of the barracks gymnasium; and all male members of the community share a dread of him. But, in mistreating Awkward John, his most docile and least wily recruit, Sergeant Cooper eventually causes his own embarrassment and loses his wife to a lover. The fleetest British soldier cannot outstrip Awkward John, who jumps ditches, bogs, and flax dams and leaves the pursuing sergeant floating in the stench of retting flax. The army's strict regimentation, which uses the sergeant's only talent, never parallels the town's easy, relaxed, humor; the sergeant's loss of dignity and of wife occurs because the army does not recognize those differences. " 'What else could you expect,' said Yellow Willy, 'if you let the like of Awkward John into the army.' "

II   *Of Love Gone Amiss*

In treating love as a theme, Kiely uses the North Ireland and Dublin settings with varying results. He has personally conducted many visitors on the tour described in "Rich and Rare Were the Gems She Wore," [6] a title also taken from a familiar ballad; and his acquaintance with the clergy enables him to write with ease and compassion the beautiful and funny story "A Great God's Angel Standing." [7]

Pride occasions the disappointment of the two heroines of "Rich and Rare Were the Gems She Wore" and "The Bright Graves": [8] pride in being a "nice girl" for Fanny in the first story, and pride in choosing a man of refinement for Elizabeth in the second one. Asked to show an American major around the city of Dublin on the eve of his departure for battle, Fanny, conducting him on a historical tour of Dublin—the Nelson Pillar, the Book of Kells, the National Library of James Joyce fame, and Howth Head—finds him charming but with effort keeps herself primly proper, recoils in shock when he presses his hotel-room key into her hand, loses the conquest to an unworthy streetwalker, and ends in doubt and confusion about the virtue of virtue.

Elizabeth of "The Bright Graves"—bright because the Irish graves are covered with gleaming white gravel—spends much of her time kneeling over the grave of a rejected lover, rejected because he was a little too big and noisy, though not uncouth. He died by accident shortly after her refusal to marry him. Kneeling by an opposite grave, another man attracts her attention; she creates an unfounded fantasy about his mourning a cherished wife only to learn, when the man's language becomes coarse and vehement, that the grave shelters the body of a despised sister. Unable to reconcile imagined ideals with crass reality, and feeling herself kissed in indecorous, angry defiance of the dead sister, Elizabeth rejects the second suitor. She returns to daydreaming about her experiences with the first big man; only in daydreams can she fortify herself against the merely human.

If "The Bright Graves" indicates a reason for spinsterhood, "Ten Pretty Girls" [9] offers an explanation of bachelorhood. Andrew Fox returns from a visit to Belfast with a story of having met exactly ten desirable young beauties and having lost all of them. The exigencies of city travel which require changing buses and trains while protecting women and staying near a boxed champion greyhound (the pride and mark of a rural man) certainly confirm his bachelorhood, though afterwards he yearns for the lost opportunities.

In the "Enchanted Palace," [10] literally a local cinema, Jack MacGowan and his friend observe romance on three levels: a film version of the Cupid and Psyche story in which a shattered war-torn hero and an ugly girl fall in love; a real romance brewing between Hughie, new from the country and for the first time in a theater, and Bridget, a town girl who shows him how the theater seat works; and a romance repulsed by Katy, a quiet and wealthy local prostitute who is approached in the darkness by a hunchback. When last seen, Katy is driving milk cows on her father's farm, having removed herself from all approaches. The ugliness of the warped body can be overlooked, even miraculously transformed by love, only when there is a corresponding beauty of soul.

In "A Great God's Angel Standing" Kiely uses an incident he witnessed when a madman confessed his sins to a black-suited layman of doubtful repute. Also, Kiely possesses a small volume of love poetry, beautifully bound and engraved and inscribed by a young woman to a priest. For some time, he meditated the mystery behind the gift of love poetry to a celibate priest and then wrote it into the story of a character he calls Pascal Stakelum, and whom he makes a notorious rural rake. An inseparable, though unlikely, companion of the gentle, serene Father Paul, who is chaste in thought and action, Pascal lives the antithesis of all that Father Paul stands for—except when a madman mistakes Pascal for a priest. Then Pascal, culling from forgotten childhood the proper words and from observation of Father Paul the proper gestures, so reverently completes the ceremony that he subdues into silence the once-jeering keeper of the mental hospital. While making the rounds of the hospital with Father Paul, Pascal arranges a rendezvous with a nurse. After Paul dies, Pascal as narrator tells the story of Paul's gift to him of a book of love poetry by William Morris inscribed to Paul with love by a girl in Virginia. In one poem, a great god's angel standing by a bed holds a blue cloth for hell and a red cloth for heaven. Pascal ponders the mixing of the symbolism at the same time that he ponders the mystery of the chaste Father Paul's lost love.

In "A Ball of Malt and Madame Butterfly," [11] Kiely blends two favorite themes: the literary and historic past of his country, and the literary-minded character who quotes poetry to unappreciative and uninformed acquaintances. A very moving portrait of the silver-haired Yeats and an observed meeting of him and the elderly Maud Gonne inspires in pinched and celibate Pike Hunter the desire to regard one of Dublin's geisha girls called Madame Butterfly as the incarnation of ideal feminine love and beauty. Usurping her time from other customers while paying her irregularly for her time because he wants their relationship to be poetic rather than mercenary, Pike soon quarrels with, and loses, his Madame Butterfly. When the keeper of the Dark Cow passes on, the fatherly fireman Austin McDonnell tells Butterfly the story of Lord Nelson, now on a pillar, who took for mistress a "slavey" [servant girl] who became his Lady Emma Hamilton. Ironically, Butterfly, inspired by the romance, rises to respectable marriage with a docker; the poetic Pike Hunter, having loved and lost, descends into lonely alcoholism. A delightfully humorous, somewhat bawdy story, it honors both the Maupassant and operatic influences suggested by its title.

III *The Printed Word*

A genuine love of books motivates a writer to take one of two positions: veneration of books and authors or harassment of those who misuse either for self-aggrandizement.

In "The Heroes in the Dark House," [12] the heroes of Irish folk tales are written about by an old scholar named Arthur Broderick, who, in the progress of the story, proves himself a hero of a special kind. Because of his own love of the stories themselves, he has nine times sent them away for printing and nine times had them rejected and returned. For a few brief days he labored over them with footnotes to augment the understanding of the garrisoned United States Army whose young men could read them in pamphlets. Then one morning, before publication, he awoke to find that the army's orders had been changed; they had vanished "like snow off a ditch." Learning, by way of a newspaper, that a young scholar who had visited him—had shared the heavy tobacco smoke in his dark home, had received his hospitality, and had gone on his way—had appropriated the stories and published them under his own name, Broderick passes through the town, communing with the sights and the people. "No young man can steal from you what you want to give away," a familiar statue seems to speak to him. In the midst of what would have been a crushing blow to most authors, Broderick's gentle humor and sympathy come out in passages of skillfully written conversation. He invites the plagiarizing young scholar, who never admits the theft, to return to continue the talks of stories they shared. Truly magnanimous, Broderick in perfect serenity gives the stories—his children—life above the signature of a stranger.

The poet of "Blackbird on a Bramble Bough" [13] meets, in contrast, ignominious defeat. Sailing under false colors of undeserved praise, he writes lyrics for undiscerning readers about a country life he never led. Paid to read the poetry of a minor poetess to a captive audience of schoolgirls, he afterward drinks the porter included in the narrator's unwilling hospitality; enlists the aid of the narrator to carry a heavy bag filled ostensibly with books but in reality with whiskey; and allows himself, drunk and roaring, to be driven in circular fashion to a back door of the "hotel," actually the local convent. His host, seeking the last drop of revenge, sinks the suitcase of liquor in the nearest bog.

Ignorance that is willfully disguised as understanding seems to be the bane of scholarly existence. In "Mon Ami, Emile," [14] the narrator, returned from the Continent and penniless, finds expected funds not delivered but enjoys the local color, especially a sign carrying the message "Meet the best people at the Amusement Palace." Savoring the irony, he sells his three volumes of Rousseau to the manager of the Amusement Palace bookstall, acts the role of thief in a den of thieves, and allows the manager to think that French literature means risqué literature.

"The Little Wrens and Robins" [15] is a vignette of Cousin Ellen of Omagh, famous for nonstop talking and for the reading of her poetry of doubtful quality from the pulpit by her soul mate, the celibate parish priest. Influenced by the painting of Burns called "The Muse of Poetry Descends to Robert Burns while at the Plough," her poetic images of springtime when daffodils put on their gowns and when "The little wrens and robins/ To all you bring good cheer" are no more fantastic and stilted than the nightgowned girl who hovers two feet above Burns's plow horses.

[46]

Nor is the impossibility of artistic achievement sadder than the delusions of more conventional and less laughable personages whose lives in their own ways all make bad art: the narrator, forgetful of letters and prone to send Ellen's suitcase to the wrong town; Ellen's gentle mother disconcertingly famous for her powerfully destructive home-brewed port wine; the uncle, unmindful of immigrant laws and destinations, stranded in the wrong country until his death; Ellen's husband, talked into marriage and then into oblivion; the new hired girl whose aspirations for a singing career are marred by her purple-blotched cheek. Turning the good side to the audience, as Cousin Ellen observed just before her death, would be required of the girl with the lovely voice; but its necessity cannot be avoided by any of imperfect humanity. Cousin Ellen's trite but sincere lines with remarkable precision and application recur to the mind of the narrator after her death. Birds, springtime, song, and even a touch of romanticism, visit the best of people. With charm, naïveté, and good intentions, one can do worse than write poor poetry.

"The Little Bishop" [16] concerns the antics of Jeremiah Slattery, a seminarian turned newspaperman who cannot eat and cannot get warm. Hating the cameraman and resenting both His Grace the Irish bishop and the visiting American bishop who require newspaper coverage of their sojourn to the Isle of the Blest, Jeremiah takes all his misery with him on a sodden stormy boat trip, during which he sees the cameraman snubbed by the bishop and observes the respected clergy cowering and praying in the "for'ard foxhole." Jeremiah, who stands at the mast without benefit of oilskin, weathers the gale as bravely as the lifeboat's skilled crew; and, finding himself a man after all, he leaves his steaming greatcoat behind, thus symbolically shedding his old self, and he returns to the mainland a new man. In the course of the visit, the American bishop has baptized and named a child for himself, and speculation about successive "Little Bishops" provides numerous quips for the dinner table. Jeremiah's corresponding baptism in the day's downpour marks his farewell to his seminary failure and to his resentment of clergy; he emerges from the incident with new self-recognition as a successful reporter.

IV *The Past Recalled*

A search for one's own origins or for the glories of a lost youth brings the past into the present and aids the understanding of the present. A conversation after the death of the father in "Wild Rover No More" [17] discloses to a small boy in hiding the origins of his parents' romance and the reasons for his mother's attachment to Hannah the Saint, a daft old beggar who believes herself the Mother of God. The story arouses the old questions of circumstance and environment: Was the father a "wild rover" in his youth because he woke up one morning with a hangover and found himself in the British army? Did Hannah lose her reason and give birth to a simple daughter because of her misuse and abandonment by a worthless husband? The child listening in hiding had never known his father as a wild rover, but he had heard many tales about the army days; neither had he known the crazy woman in her youth as the village Queen of the May. It is the child's first experience with what might have been—had circumstances been different.

"The Dogs in the Great Glen" [18] tells about an American's search in Ireland for the home of his grandfather. Part of the experience Kiely tells as one of his own favorite stories: the visit of himself and Kevin Sullivan to Lady Gregory's Coole Park, the scene of Yeats's poem "The Wild Swans at Coole," and their watching rise from the water exactly the number of swans mentioned in the poem. The remainder of the story tells how, when the two visitors arrived at the little-known Glen of Kanareen, the huge dogs, usually hostile to strangers, let them pass as if they were known and soon they are greeted by the grandfather's brother who recognized the American visitor from afar by his gait. Timelessness is the theme, as if the people change no more than does the rocky countryside.

"A Walk in the Wheat" [19] tells about the return of a man to the land of his youth with an American-born daughter seemingly out of place because she wears slacks, hitherto unknown in the valley. But, amid old jokes and folk tales told as they walk, she sees through the mist a man walking around a rock, a man no one else can see, as if he is the reincarnation of the old hermit of their tales. She, too, has an inherited appreciation and sense of belonging to a country she has never before seen.

In "The Weavers at the Mill," [20] a Canadian newswoman visits an old man in order to write a magazine story about the old man's heroism in a sea disaster off Ireland's shore. She and the old man develop heartfelt rapport—and spend the last day together holding hands, despite the antagonism of the man's wife—though the newswoman is short of thirty and the hero nearly eighty. Over the gateway a decayed sculptured phoenix symbolizes the decay of the fine old hero. She leaves, "taking his second youth with her, towing the sailing islands behind her. She was the sea receding for ever from a stranded master of the sea. . . . She walked on under the stone phoenix that could never rise again because it had simply decayed, never been purified by fire and burned to ashes." [21]

V   *In Youth Is Wonder*

To understand the past, one may also recall the adventures of childhood, especially the crucial period of adolescence when the child grows out of innocence; often experiences pain, embarrassment, and disillusionment; but invariably acquires new knowledge, dignity, and awareness of self. Such is the experience of Isaac when an untamed horse bought by Tansey, the carter in the story "The White Wild Bronco," [22] becomes the symbol of all unrealized dreams—for the cowboy who has never seen Wyoming, but talks about it and watches the taming of the bronco, and for small Isaac who dreams of coaxing it to gentleness with sugar lumps and love. Tansey, who strikes the animal between the eyes with a crowbar, unceremoniously tames it; but for Isaac, who is watching and listening, the adult conversation suddenly takes on strange new overtones. Isaac's father tells him the cowboy has never been out of town, though he has a bow-legged walk, a Stetson hat, and dozens of Western stories. Isaac learns to listen as the adults do, tolerating the fantasies of others, pretending to accept them as reality, and seeing the idiosyncrasies of the town's many beloved citizens, along with their dreams, as necessary for worthwhile living.

"A View from the Treetop" [23] combines two themes—history and children. The child Paddy experiences an important step in the process of individuation by climbing a tree to escape detection as the thief of the Old Master's treasured musket balls. From his high perch, he watches the town life a whole day, realizing "he could really think and size things up and get control of life by sitting up in the lime tree and meditating." He descends once to eat a roasted pheasant being carried to the inspector as a gift from the young teacher's wife; and, after the fury dies down, he learns, after appropriate punishment and repayment, that the kind Old Master had always known where the musket balls were, had known Paddy was in the tree, and had let the child make his own decisions in his own time. Echoing Paddy's discovery, the Old Master says, "Climbing up on high, Paddy, a man comes closer to himself." Like an unsung Robert Frost, he adds, "I knew you couldn't go far astray if you were merely closer to heaven than anybody else in the village: thinking your own thoughts."

"The Pilgrims" [24] develops from another theme important in Kiely's writing: religion. The hero is again a child, painfully aware of adult imposition upon him of a child's short pants; and his friend George makes him even more painfully aware of his inexperience with women. At age thirteen, he shivers "on the threshold of knowledge" when he realizes that George and Rosaleen have contrived a rendezvous by escaping from mass; shortly after, he gazes into the water under a bridge, "losing his own identity in the movement of the blue water." Returning from the pilgrimage to the water's edge, he tastes the first kiss of a girl to whom he is drawn because she, too, was rejected by George. Throughout the story, the boy's consciousness of the intensity of colors signals his approaching new awareness; after the rebirth experience, he interprets them: blue is the rosary and the coat of a laughing girl; black is night and "mouth finding mouth in the darkness and making a beginning and an end."

"The House in Jail Square" [25] identifies a house which is, in itself, a jail for a schoolboy who rooms there with its two spinster owners as his jailers. Until he sees his keepers mortified by a school chum, he accepts their grotesque tyranny, runs their errands to place bets on horses, peels their potatoes, allows them to make his treasured stone marker from the jail into a flower stand, and listens to their threats and insults. Between loyalty to his mother, whose childhood friends they were, and the ridicule of his schoolmates, he wavers uncomfortably; finally, he precipitates his release from the spinsters by baptizing them with a glass of lemonade in the face poured from a stairwell above. But freedom and maturity bring guilt for having abandoned "childless ageing women whose way of life was charted in loneliness and shadows."

The ways of the adults remain ever mysterious to the child. "The Wild Boy" [26] tells about Lanty, who leads his boyhood friend, the narrator, on a delightful holiday of fishing for stickle-backs and of chasing bees that ends almost disastrously too close to dynamite in the stone quarries. The child recognizes Lanty's worth and sense of responsibility when Lanty refuses to let him wade in deep water for "blackheads"—the child's name for cat-tails. But the narrator's mother firmly rescues him from the company of the wild Lanty and dynamite. Years later, when Lanty, a war-torn hero, and the aged mother are patients in the same hospital, the narrator returns to the subject of Lanty's character, expecting it to require defense. The mother has no awareness of previous doubts about him. "Isn't it wonderful the way his wound bleeds?" she asks. "Just like his father before him. His father, God be good to him, was a fine man."

Two familiar themes of Irish literature are woven into "Homes on the Mountain": [27] the returned American, and the famous lengthy Irish courtship. The godmother and godfather of young Tommy return from America to build a house in an unlikely but picturesque spot near the nearly destroyed remains of a fine home inhabited by two old bachelor brothers, John and Thady O'Neill. Hermitic and repulsive, they have simplified their existence to eating boiled potatoes from an overcoat-covered table and to sleeping in one huge four-poster bed. The child, watching them and listening to his father talk to them, cannot imagine the hunched, decrepit figures engaged in activities of lovemaking and in living with "wild" army men. When the visitors return to the godmother's house, the adults laugh because the children who cannot sing buy songbooks to read songs; but the child's odd reasoning seems no more illogical than that of either adult family, of the fine returned Americans who built a house in a nearly inaccessible spot on a mountainside, or of the lonely old man who courted sixty years without marrying and descended with his brother into living like animals.

Only children and the most reverend of the clergy are close enough to heaven to accept the slightly odd as part of humanity and to be accepted in return. Together, the three types form a special brotherhood. Big May of "The Shortest Way Home" [28] will consent to walk with pesky younger brothers because she has the simplicity and the curiosity of a child and goes, therefore, by long and devious routes, for pleasures which they gratefully share. The Wee Brother accepts into his fold at the Christian Brothers School a child too young and too small for his class as cheerfully as he accepts the highly individualistic four he calls the Four Horsemen of the Apocalypse. Under the guidance of such rare individuals as Big May and the Wee Brother, the children perform such senseless tasks as gathering nettles for tea and as copying meaningless sentences—"I would give you some violets but they withered when my father died"—for writing practice. The protectors of children allow them freedom for risqué adventures and freedom for individuality—and hold them loosely until the meaningless becomes meaningful. An irate old woman flailing a butcher knife over the bowed head of her husband brings from May a scornful, "From what they say she couldn't cut a slice of bread," and the line remains in memory to frighten away many an adult bogey. From the man too short and the woman too tall, the child learns about human values not measured by school grades or by material possessions. Not the number of footsteps but the number of rich pleasures determines the best way home.

"A Bottle of Brown Sherry" [29] tells how two thirteen-year-old boys witness a scene of moonlight lovemaking and understand, all at once, why Mr. Edward had an operation, why a barebreasted Juno adorns the highest pipe of the organ, why old John talks to the flagstones he lays as if they were women, why in a conspicuous spot in the hall hangs a picture of Mr. Edward's brother with a bear he shot as fitting demonstration of his virility, and why the spinster Miss Grania performs something like a fertility rite in the process of selecting lobsters for dinner. While drunk on a secretly purchased bottle of brown sherry, swaying gently in the top of a favorite pine tree, the boys watch surgically revitalized Edward perform with a servant maid in the role of bare-breasted Juno. Their fathers' commands bring down to earth two sick but newly informed young men who now, because they can put together a number of observations, understand more about adult life than the Edward and Juno scene alone revealed.

From self-conscious embarrassment to cathartic laughter, the adolescent progresses on a journey to Dublin and return in "A Cow in the House." [30] Before the journey begins, a haircut by the local barber who keeps a cow in his house leaves the boy bald and subject to the ridicule of his friends; in Dublin, a loose heel on his shoe increases his discomfiture as he clacks through the streets; a visit to a convent adds to his torment when, pressed to sing, in confusion he chooses and sings a bawdy song for the nuns. A visit to the hall of mirrors marks the turning point; he emerges laughing, for he realizes that all people are in some way caricatures. All have "big noses, red faces, legs too long or short, behinds that waggled, clothes that didn't fit. Every one of them had a cow in the house." "A Cow in the House" tells a personal experience of Kiely's youth on his first trip to Dublin. Years later, as he related to his friend Brendan Behan all his childhood embarrassment about the bald head and clacking shoe, he concluded: "I thought all Dublin was watching me." Brendan Behan, who must have been six years old at the time, quipped, "They were. I was watching you meself."

"A Journey to the Seven Streams" [31] marks an attempt by a home-loving father to take his family to the scenes of his youth; he relates the myths, geography, and history of the area as they travel. The doubtful conveyance offered by Hookey Baxter's erratic old car, which requires pushing up hill and which threatens its passengers with imminent explosion, adds humor and wit to the journey and also guarantees the destination will not be reached. More than a journey into the past, though the father provides a running travelogue, the trip focuses on the personalities of car and driver, father and mother. The trip is a reminiscence about the father's past, but it occasions for the adult narrator many years later similar reminiscences about his own past.

CHAPTER 4

The Shrouded Present:
Land Without Stars

V IRTUALLY engulfed in quiet except for the spasmodic roar
of war planes overhead, the Northern Ireland community of
Kiely's first novel, *Land Without Stars*, projects the tripartite
vulnerability of an essentially peaceful people. They are, in the
years 1940–41, as the Kerry poet Egan O'Rahilly more than two
centuries before described them in his native Gaelic, occupants
of "a land without dry weather, without a stream, without a star." [1]
Kiely's crossing the length of the island to pluck an epigraph from
the work of a Southern poet is an example of what Sean Mc-
Mahon has called Kiely's "mischievous rearrangement of topog-
raphy," [2] but the mixing of the Dublin and Northern Ireland settings is even more obvious in the totality of Kiely's work. *Land
Without Stars* more poignantly than any other of his novels
focuses on the national questions of Protestantism versus Catholicism, of geographic and political division versus the ideal of a
united Ireland, and of Gaelic versus English as a national language.

I *The Present Conflicts*

At the time of *Land Without Stars*, World War II casts darkness over the British Isles. While Northern Ireland's soldiers fight
with Britain against Germany, the Republic of Ireland remains
neutral. The novel, then, chronicles perhaps nine months in the
lives of two brothers who, at the beginning, return to their Northern Ireland home for the Christmas holidays. Davy Quinn arrives
from the North, his brother Peter from the South, both to find
the town crouching behind blackout blinds.

Peter, a clerical student, quietly opposes Davy's Irish Republican idealism and guards himself against the charms of Rita
Keenan, who tempestuously assails his pride and his devotion

to his mother. At seminary, Peter's growing doubt about the sincerity of his calling finally determines his withdrawal from the priesthood, but on his return home he finds Rita Keenan engaged to his brother Davy who is increasingly involved with the outlaw Dick Slevin. The involvement soon makes both Davy and Dick outlaws; and Rita, confessing her love for Peter, determines to break her engagement to Davy. She does so just minutes before a wary policeman shoots Davy as he barely misses a train which would have carried him to freedom. Slevin escapes; Peter leaves for Dublin, still friends with Rita; but with Davy dead, something of the love between Rita and Peter has died also.

II *Passion and Power*

Peter's attraction to one of the "dark quiet ones," or, as Rita is also described, one of the "shrouded few," augments the theme of the uncertain present. Because she forebodes the darkness of evil, should the end of the story indicate a heretofore unknown direction and improved purpose in Peter's existence, he must go to Dublin without Rita. The symbolism of the desirable dark girl, ultimately left behind, and its link to the red and white flowers becomes obvious: both kinds of flowers grow in front of the house that is now a seminary.[3] The white of purity, chastity, and innocence suggests the ideals of men training for celibate priesthood. But it is impossible to weed out of the nature of virulent young men some awareness at least of the lusty red flowers of passion. In the novel, cultivation of their springtime bloom occupies Brother Dowdall at the time he sees a stray holiday couple kiss. Also, the withering of the red blossoms explains Peter's friend Jacob's sixty-year courtship that culminated not in marriage but in death. Peter's confusion between the clerical and the secular life is the recognition that both flowers grow side by side; both are lovely, and both are God's work. The "evil" of passion, appropriately with a dark-haired girl, and the darkness of criminal evil divide Peter's rationality and also oppress him who attempts to live God's life in a man's world. When Davy's death, the result of affiliation with evil, thrusts itself between him and the "thin dark girl," the forced withdrawal without her points the way to a new future. There is, in his trip to Dublin, the sadness of loss, a running away from something desirable, and also a running toward the future.

The dominant image of *Land Without Stars* is a damaged statue of Diana which stands in the garden of the country home that has been converted to a Jesuit college.[4] It is not merely the incongruity of a pagan statue in a Roman Catholic setting which preys on the mind of Peter Quinn and not merely the goddess of chastity placed among red flowers but the permanent sneer on her face, resulting from a chance shattering of her nose, that symbolizes imperfection in individual character and, on another level, the scars of a nation. The preservation of her damaged condition indicates the vanity and vain pretense toward perfection, shaped by the sculptor, as well as the vain ideals both of patriots and of men of God. Thus, the statue of Diana as a symbol unifies the religious and political themes of the book.

A Greek temple across a weedy lake at the Jesuit college also imposes the pagan past upon the Christian present, and near it a sculptured Actaeon runs from sculptured hounds. Diana, an impotent goddess, gazes upon pursued and pursuers and sneers. These images of the petrified past gradually fade into the background as Peter becomes increasingly engrossed in secular life after he leaves the college; but, as he ponders his relationship with Rita, to whom his brother is engaged, he remembers an earlier experience.

The recurring image is that of two girls running to catch the Belfast express. At the time the incident occurred, Peter and Jim Carson shouted at them to jump down the bank. Here again is chastity pursued by desire, succumbing at last amid the high warm grasses of a railroad bank, for Peter's first love experience.

The unwary innocent and good are always liable to manipulations by the unprincipled. This Peter senses, and Davy the idealist fails to realize. Though the story is told primarily in the third person through Peter's view and in chronological order, Chapter II entitled "Davy," and Chapter III entitled "Peter" are told in the first person from the viewpoint of each character, respectively. Chapters II and III in this way set forth the differences in the personalities of the two brothers as they explain themselves and each other. Davy fails to appreciate the depth of Peter's thinking, the range and diversity of Peter's viewpoint. Kiely sets forth Davy's view with meticulous care. Davy's failure to probe beneath the surface of a casual remark and his acceptance of it at face value consistently reappear. He does not, for example, observe that Rita never tells him she loves him. He does not realize she talks about ghosts because of what she sees of Peter in him. He is deliriously happy with her promise to marry him; that happiness is enough.

Though Peter and Davy love the same girl, the contention between them is generally political; and from Chapter V to the end, the novel is essentially Peter's thoughtful commentary about Davy's political activities. The setting is one of constant tension, frequent alerts, and nightly blackouts. Feeling about the war is divided because of internal political strife over the Partition. Those who hate Britain and oppose the Partition are optimistically misled about the intentions of Germany. The contrasting characters of the brothers, then, reflect national differences.

III *People and Politics*

Dissension between brothers, which is at once the most dramatic and disheartening aspect of civil war, provides in *Land Without Stars* the clearest insight into the character of Ireland; like many of their countrymen, the ideals of Davy and Peter Quinn are as sharply different as their personalities are.

The brothers are most sharply divided on the question of politics. Glibly quoting a slogan originated by Padraic Pearse, Davy says "Ireland unfree and partitioned would never be at peace." Peter replies, "The I.R.A. are antagonistic to both Church and State." Their political divergence extends into religious and leisure activities: Davy refuses to go to the movies because "The King" is played at the end; instead, he attends Gaelic League classes; to him, Gaelic is a good in itself. At home, while Peter reads his missal, Davy reads *The Principles of Freedom*. Peter's bedtime ritual is the recitation of prayer; Davy's is the examination of a gun.

Davy, the man who works with his hands, thinks with his heart. Because of his ardent desire for a united Ireland, he regards the Partition and the union with Great Britain as the only verifiable and tangible evil. Whatever serves either to unify Ireland or to sever ties with Britain will, assuredly, obtain his active and wholehearted support. That such an extreme position usually necessitates some compromises in ethics Davy would never realize. To him, good and evil know no variables. "Black's black and white's white," he says.

Practically, Davy avoids conflict by compartmentalizing. The values of religion, for example, have no bearing on war. Though prayer is a virtue at home, a general is not to be admired for praying or reading his Bible while at war. Davy maintains the Dutch lost the Boer War because "What Kruger wanted was a wee book on revolutionary method. How to blow up things." [5] In the present conflict, his sympathy is with Germany. "I'll change the world, Mother," he says. "Change our lives and give freedom to Ireland. The weight will fall off from the shoulders of humanity" (75). A nation to believe in is any enemy of Britain, and a friend to trust is anyone who has broken the laws of Britain. Thus Jack Carney aptly describes Davy as "radical, revolutionary, and Irish republican." Peter characterizes Davy as "plain, direct, forcible, firm as his handshake, the honest glance of his eyes. . . . Davy could know nothing of the turning and twisting of any mind that did not like his own, leap to conclusions, accept shibboleths, simplify life to a struggle between Right and Might, the valiant Green against the mighty Red. For Davy, Prussian boots covered feet beautiful upon the mountains. His own personal problems were lost in great generalisations, unsolved, unsolvable" (14).

Peter has greater knowledge but less certainty than Davy. Peter's keen perception and his appreciation of many writers enable him to supply readily a pertinent quotation for every conceivable situation. But, for Peter, just as examination of many authors provides diversity of viewpoint, so examination of his own conscience reveals the manifold and conflicting aspects of his being. His calling demands certainty and singleness of devotion, but he will never have either; he thinks too much.

Personally, the calling has subdued and refined Peter's behavior. He has learned, for example, to cut his bread neatly on the side plate; but education, that is, the willingness to learn, ultimately requires one to assume the position, "I question." Religion, on the other hand, requires one to assume the position, "I accept." What voice speaks to Peter? "My conscience? The devil?" he asks and answers, at the time of leaving the college, "I'll never know. That's the trouble with people like me. We never know" (60). And several months later Peter still questions. Brother Jones apparently knows what God wants for him, but Peter does not know "how he was to know when God did or did not want his servant, Peter Quinn, to take possession of this, that or the other thing" (181).

Just as Peter's calling has not successfully channeled his riotous thoughts, neither has it ascertained automatically any advantages in human relationships. The attitudes of others toward him are altered only according to the respect they hold for his office. Simply, a priest officiates at christenings, at weddings, at funerals —the giving of life, of love, of eternity. Among people who value these ceremonies, the black clothes set Peter apart from the rest of society and earn him preferential treatment. When he crosses the border, he observes the customs officer apprise his attire, courteously make the chalk mark, and pass by. His friends Arthur Williams and Jim Carson, as they walk down the street, place him in the center "as a mark of honour to the Church"; and Peter observes that "noisy talk and noisy jokes" are carefully toned down in his presence.

But the Christmas Day visit with Pete and Jacob, when Peter and Davy meet the evil Dick Slevin, and the subsequent reunion with Rita, demonstrate the ineffectualness of good clerical intentions. In the provinces of love and lawlessness, the black cloth provides no barrier, no defense, not even a zone of neutrality for those irrational forces.

The Irish Republican Army activities of Davy and Peter's teacher friend, Jim Carson, automatically affiliate them, sincere and well intentioned as they are, with the outlaw Dick Slevin, who opposes the British government for personal reasons. Jim Carson, maintaining somewhat like Peter a quiet and dispassionate rationality, can evaluate the relative merits of Slevin's character; but Davy's idealism makes him blind to the essential evil of his friend. Davy's relationship with Slevin is the alliance of innocence with evil for a patriotic ideal.

Slevin thrives on civil war because it offers an excuse for violence, cunning, and excitement. He engages in such prosaic revolutionary activities as blowing up bridges. Deported from England, he is hounded by the police in British North Ireland; but he honestly tries to impress upon Davy that his love for Ireland is "purely negative." Dick Slevin calls himself an outlaw; Davy insists that he and Slevin are soldiers. Slevin attempts to clarify his position: "You want to see Ireland free, whatever you mean by that. I don't give a curse. If Ireland were free tomorrow

I'd be where I am, see? On the run. Fellows like me are always on the run." When Davy insists he also hates the police, Slevin replies, "But you hated them because they represented England. I hated them because they represented law, any law, see?" (90).

In spite of Slevin's honesty, Davy fails to understand that Slevin, who hates British law, does not also embrace the alternative love, the ideal of a united Ireland. Peter remembers Davy's ecstatic description of his one trip to Dublin; it is a description based on selected and temporary details. Contrary to Davy's report, the sun does not always shine in Dublin; the foam-tossed waters of the Liffey must occasionally float refuse; the sound of Irish must be mixed with English; and the national anthem certainly is not sung twenty-four hours a day! Peter's comment is: "Poor Davy. Would he ever learn?"

But the kind of Ireland which Davy imagines, and the kind which is the objective of contemporary politics, almost exists at the vacation spot in Donegal. This setting and this experience are remote from the war, both with Britain and with Germany. It provides a view of the ideal Ireland envisioned by Pearse when he described in 1915 the Ireland of the future as "not free merely, but Gaelic as well; not Gaelic merely, but free as well." [6]

At the Rosses of Donegal, a bit of Ireland is set aside by the benefactor Father Murray, who in reality founded the nearby college for the study of Gaelic and where Kiely himself learned Gaelic. Here the novel pictures shawled local women amid a rural setting of donkeys and sheep, a cluster of whitewashed houses with gray roofs sloping down to the sea edged with ragged, gray, spray-washed rocks, and the sunshine and the mists and the good-natured companionship of people who live from nature rather than from competition with one another. In the homes and in the college only Gaelic is spoken.

Peter calls it fanaticism, to insist upon Gaelic Ireland, and Carson defends it because "Ireland could have no consistent, coherent future if Irish men and women were ignorant of their past. . . . The very foundations of nationhood rested on such apparently trivial things as the remnants of bardic verse" (105). Forced to study it, Peter eventually learns to appreciate Gaelic literature as literature, though not for politics.

In addition to the varying viewpoints about language, *Land Without Stars* shows the pub as the center of social life since it provides opportunity for long discussions and also for singing time-honored songs in which Ireland is represented as an old woman paying her rent and yearning to live on her own land. To Peter, such songs evoke painful memories of past famine and emigration. But there are also the lighthearted songs, some with bawdy verses; and there are stories told with the same themes.

Ironically, besides the misuse of literature in the name of patriotism, another misused power is that of Peter's calling. The appeal of the priesthood, he remembers while examining his conscience, is the power vested in the priest—a power best represented in a picture of "hands lifted in sacrifice, in forgiveness, the power to bind and loose."

Land Without Stars thus looks backward politically to *Counties of Contention* and forward religiously to *There Was an Ancient House*. In presenting the conflicting viewpoints of Davy and Peter, Kiely in this novel approaches the objectivity of his later work.

CHAPTER 5

The Springtime of the Local Life:
In a Harbour Green

THE novel *In a Harbour Green* ends, "The river flowed between dark green trees and bright green grass, towards the
grey town and the blue sea"—and in its ending as its beginning,
innocence is belied by the contents. *In a Harbour Green* in pure
irony tells about murder, robbery, suicide, an illegitimate child,
and rape in a small Northern Ireland town which stifles creativity,
slanders reputations, votes Unionist, and opposes progress. Of the
carefully drawn characters who provide insight into town life,
chief among them are sophisticated Bernard Fiddis; the proper
and righteous Aunt Aggie Campbell; the blossoming young
woman, May Campbell; her innocent sister, Dympna; the football
hero, Jim Collins; the town bully, Bear Mullan; the affectionate
father, John Campbell; the alcoholic loose woman, Alice Graham;
and the murderer, John Maxwell.

I *In the Midst of Life*

As the story begins, John Maxwell has been tried for, and freed
of, charges of murdering his wife. Then other problems and
mysteries develop: Chris Collins and Dinny Campbell find a
stolen antique sword; Aunt Aggie Campbell suffers a paralyzing
stroke. Brass MacManus and Pat Rafferty, driving Maxwell home
from a fair day, hear his drunken confession of murder. Chris
Collins and Dinny Campbell stumble upon the hideout of the
Bear Mullan and his friends in an abandoned house. May Campbell learns about love with Bernard Fiddis.

In a snowstorm, Joe Keenan, Bear Mullan, and Gerry Campbell
stop at the house where Lizzie is the maid; she becomes
enamoured of Gerry Campbell. Bear Mullan plans to rob the
place, and he once more confirms the community's poor opinion

of him by attempting to take a sled from the small boys, Chris Collins and Dinny Campbell. Pat Rafferty intervenes, but these low-key attempts at petty crimes persist. One night Fiddis discovers Gerry Campbell robbing his house. Soon after, Fiddis and Rafferty set out on a flood-rescue mission on a raft, but they find that the occupants of endangered houses prefer not to be rescued, and the mission proves utterly futile. Subsequently, May Campbell realizes her pregnancy by Pat Rafferty; and, after much anxiety and whispered discussions among family and community, Fiddis asks her to marry him. Lizzie is attacked by a mystery man; Gerry Campbell just as mysteriously disappears. Joe Keenan and Pat Rafferty pursue the Bear Mullan and extort his confession of both crimes. The Bear, having lost face and given over tyranny in his homeland, leaves for England. Another desperate and lonely person is Alice Graham, who tells Pat Rafferty that May has been wantonly promiscuous; Fiddis, for Pat's benefit, confirms the story and receives without protest Pat's blow on the chin. Pat enlists and drowns accidentally at sea while May and Fiddis, with the child, form the picture of an ideal family.

II *Town Life through a Window*

These are the activities motivated by conflicting emotions behind the peaceful scenes of gray houses and blue sea. Writing for the 1944 *Capuchin Annual*, Kiely describes a penholder miniature of Errigal and adds, "The confirmed tourist sees those pictures, only those pictures. But a thousand men and a thousand women might look through those pictures as through a windowpane or a transparent veil, looking into another world, seeing Donegal not symbolised by this view or that view, their own Donegal made familar by something great or something trivial not to be found in Bundoran or Gweedore or Glengesh or Glenveigh." [1]

These two sentences set forth both the theme and the method of *In a Harbour Green:* the theme, because it is a story of conventional small-town life in which the measure of triviality and greatness depends upon the particular vantage point and the lack of comparisons; the method, because a brief Chapter I entitled "A Moment" describes the effort of photography to capture a moment in time and thereby create another of those misleading conventional pictures. On command, fifty-nine pupils of the Christian Brothers school momentarily hold their smiles for the photographer and, the picture taken, explode into resumed activities. The variety of possibilities suggested explains why there are eight plots in the novel; and, in this, the second novel, Kiely explores the intricacies of plot manipulation to meet the challenge of organizing diverse materials. The focus of attention moves objectively from a school scene to a street scene to a home scene to the lonely meditations of Bernard Fiddis; thereafter, the characters introduced, and numerous others who appear later, reveal subjectively their own viewpoints on nearly every phase of town life.

The novel interweaves the following plots: the destiny of the acquitted murderer, the sex experiences of May Campbell, the approaching death of Aunt Aggie, the fate of the town "bad woman," the robbery, the evil Bear Mullan, the innocent romance of Dympna Campbell and Jim Collins, and Rafferty's flood-control project. These plots involve approximately thirty-two characters, not to mention those simply called "the nurse" or "the priest." Appearances, as in the photograph, deceptively indicate among all these people some unity in purposes and practices, in morals and ideals, an even tenure of the townspeople's ways; but, from under the surface calm, their hatred, intolerance, jealousy, and pettiness emerge, taking the form sometimes of open enmity and violence. The setting at the outbreak of World War II parallels the life of the town; the smoldering hatreds and ambitions of nations seemingly at peace soon will erupt in international confrontations just as murder, robbery, rape, and violence lie shallowly beneath the surface of the usually tranquil and moral life of the town.

III The Model Town

The town assumes an identity of its own; for example, "the town knew that Alice Graham and May Campbell were as thick as thieves," [2] and the triteness of the expression fits the town's standards. Like Big Brother watching, it judges, seldom approves, but frequently condemns the actions of all those who move through and around it. They cannot escape its eyes or its judgment; at the same time, they are enslaved to it by their own sense of propriety. Even those, like May Campbell, who are most conscious of the restriction and confinement, and resent it most thoroughly, still consciously or unconsciously, through their sense of propriety, support the standards of the town.

Bernard Fiddis looms large as the one person who seemingly should be free; he does indeed associate freely with the notorious Alice Graham, but even the innocent Pat Rafferty comprehends more fully than she the exact bounds of Fiddis' freedom: "Did Alice Graham think that Bernard Fiddis would risk his livelihood and the favour of the town by marrying a foreign woman who was no better than a tramp?" (237). Fiddis' thoughts of his marriage to May Campbell are simply stated: "what the town didn't know the town couldn't talk about." So much does the town confine the proper citizens that Jim Collins complains, "Nothing to be guilty about in our town. I go to confession once a fortnight and, honest to God, I never have anything to tell. What can one do here?" (199).

The answer to Jim Collins' question emerges clearly from the unmerited predicament of the amateur artist and musician Joe Keenan. Joe scorns the Bear Mullan's tale of a girl who fiddled on the streets of Dublin and became famous. Joe retorts, "That was in Dublin. Nobody hears you in this town. I've been at this for years and who ever heard me that was worth the dung on his boots? . . . There isn't a wall in the town that I haven't drawn something on. But who ever made a remark on them except the poxy sergeant that threatened to clink me if he caught me drawing any more girls in bathing suits. Disfiguring the town, he said, with naked women" (211).

Actually, disfigurement of the town comes from the very activities of living which the town wishes to protect. The section of town called Crawford's Alley, where Joe Keenan lives, he ironically terms the hanging gardens of Babylon: "a desolate expanse of black grassless clay, spotted with occasional heaps of stones and rusted tin cans, criss-crossed with fences of sagging wire" (251).

The apparent contradictions in the identification of the town best explain its narrow nature. Because the town talks too much, what the town does not know, it cannot talk about. Those who are most sensitive, most resentful, and most intelligent are they who most cherish the virtue of reticence. This reticence also explains why murder and violence and rape occur at the same time that Jim Collins claims there is nothing to confess. The person who had suffered most, Bear Mullan, paradoxically has withheld information—what he saw Bernard Fiddis and May Campbell doing in a parked car—when it would seem natural for him to expose those in an eminently enviable position. The desire for freedom, along with awareness of restraint, encourages, not freedom, but more restraint.

On the surface, concern for propriety best characterizes the town's citizenry; [3] but there dwells underneath propriety a basic respect for human decency—though this respect too is ironic. It is a respect best nourished by those persons whose high ideals of God and man motivate them most quickly to point out the errors of their fellows. Always people can hope for a better society; and, in the archetypal springtime of the novel's conclusion, May Campbell's baby brings new life and hope. A product of the strength and beauty of Pat Rafferty and May Campbell, he can profit from the knowledge and resources of May's husband, Bernard Fiddis. Whatever the scandal, the town will recover; time and the river flow into eternity. True, at the end, world war is imminent; but it no doubt will have little effect on a town sheltered and secure "in a harbour green."

IV *The Model Citizen*

In the small town of *In a Harbour Green,* Bernard Fiddis, age forty, provides the example of sophistication. He is not purely likable; at times, he appears unpleasantly pompous but also admirable. As a character, his self-assurance and superiority mildly antagonize; he is too complacent, too certain of his superiority to the commonplace citizenry. For example, when he learns of May Campbell's pregnancy, his mind is "perfectly quiet." At all times, his every action is meditated; he is never uncomfortably startled by a miscalculation.

Having traveled to far places, as others have not, Fiddis casts a bemused, tolerant glance upon the opinions and activities of those whose affairs and thoughts are circumscribed by the boundaries of one county. He occupies himself as a solicitor, having returned home to make his home in the land he knows best. Long past the idealism of youth, he does not seek to change the world but merely to live in it. Resignation, therefore, is one key to his tolerance; sophistication is another. Having recognized the ways

of the town and the ways of the world, he defends a murderer, lets
two small boys keep a "found" sword recently stolen from his
home, withholds the identity of a thief caught in his own house,
rides a raft at floodtime on a futile rescue mission, and allows
Pat Rafferty, father of May Campbell's unborn child, to believe
May has been randomly promiscuous. That Fiddis is not well
liked appears in the conversation during the flood-rescue mission:

> "It's the solicitor from the town."
> "Begod he'll stop the floods."
> "With his fat backside."
> "He'll write a stiff letter to the man that makes the rain."
> "He'll sue God Almighty for trespass." (172)

In other scenes less dramatic than flood rescue, he is clearly
deceptive, because his deception is both calculated and altruistic
as he listens sympathetically to expressions of religious views he
does not share, accepts the tyranny of the church, contributes to
the local dramatic society for production of a limited but Mon-
signor-approved play, and hears Old Man Rafferty urging flood
control which the people will never support. At home, Fiddis
keeps an aging, sexless spinster guardian of the community's
chastity for housekeeper. Politically, he runs for office on the Nationalist [4] ticket, knowing he will be defeated.

Fiddis listens calmly to the actor Jack MacGowan relate the
Monsignor's comment about O'Casey. The Monsignor, having an
idol of his own preserve, feels compelled to desecrate a rival idol
of the contemporary theater. "The dog," he says of O'Casey,
"If he wrote the thirty-days prayer it would be a sin to say it."
Fiddis, listening, thinks of politics and playacting as "two equally
comic manifestations of life."

A liberal in all matters, then, amid the juvenile befuddlement
about sex, the youngsters call him a "gas man"; ironically, he
drives a large yellow car, a demonstration of his ability to proceed
as if to "act well the part" were life itself. The large car also symbolizes his superiority and his incongruity in the community.
Though without apparent ostentation, he makes of it a motorized
steed to bring him dashing to rescue small Dinny Campbell from
the brutality of Bear Mullan and to carry the maid May Campbell
to a tryst under a railroad bridge.

When Fiddis wearies of the scrutiny of the town and housekeeper, he considers three means of escape: a journey, Alice Graham, and his diary. Most frequently he turns to the diary to record there a series of prosaic thoughts expressed in a prosaic style. The bubble of the illusion that these thoughts, which would no doubt scandalize the town, would scandalize an uninvolved stranger breaks against his realization that: "Superiority and detachment were fragile bubbles." In the old conflict between the spirit and the flesh, he cannot remain entirely detached from involvement with May Campbell. Indeed, his protest, "No man is his own master," when he complains of his housekeeper's supervision, both endears him as a human being and demonstrates his wisdom; but, in his marriage, he proves the accuracy of the statement. The reasons he must be admired best reveal themselves in his thoughts on his approaching marriage: "How could he blame her? If she had given herself to the whole world, he had still been preferred to all the world" (246).

Generally, he regards the world compassionately from under the lowered eyelids of experience; he protects those he loves from knowledge of themselves and, in his own way, shows kindness to every person. Paradoxically, realizing as he does the imperfections of his associates, his own superiority, skepticism, and detachment are the very agents which free him from vain espousal of vain causes to let events develop naturally. Whatever is, is right. The murderer, freed by society, lives in loneliness and remorse, experiences his own punishment, and takes his own life. The unexposed thief decides to become a priest; the play production merits local, if not national, praise; the floods abate; the rapist-thief flees to England disgraced by his former friends. Acting in character, Fiddis withholds from May Campbell the final information that Pat Rafferty has died at sea. Eventually, she learns about his fate, but she never learns what Fiddis alone knows—that Pat went to sea because of her. And, in the house bereft of its only son, the memory of that son remains untarnished by awareness of his hapless fatherhood.

V   *Imminent Evil*

The Bear Mullan, who represents ugliness and fear, is the principle of evil in tangible form; the wrongs he commits against society—beatings, robbery, rape—can be identified with certainty as wrong. If, at the end, his flight to England makes him appear a sacrificial scapegoat, if the triumph in his disgrace stems from a feeling of purification with his riddance, as if the sins of the community are ridden out with him, these psychological factors of the importance of identifying and labeling evil are certainly present.

The Bear himself does not appear malicious except as brute strength compensates for inferiority; therefore, he appears a stereotype in his frequent bullying of the small boys, Chris Collins and Dinny Campbell. Physical endowments of a tall and thin frame bent forward as if growing "in a different direction," his "pointy chin, his thin face, his little eyes set too close together," along with pidgeon toes, would inspire anyone to retaliate against offending Nature by committing destructive acts. The Bear's one friend, Joe Keenan, is another oddity, for his virtuoso musical and artistic talents sprawl, untrained and unchanneled, beyond the appreciation of the townspeople. He too retaliates and also achieves perpetuity by painting nude women on nearly unscalable walls which are protected by projections from wind and rain. Gerry Campbell completes the triumvirate of the Bear and his friends; but, fair of face and innocent in intention, Gerry is frequently an unwilling companion and accomplice. His timidity as well as his fairness of features wins him the epithet "pansy." Later he determines to withdraw, to become a priest.

In a deserted and, by repute, "haunted" house, these three have created a Tom Sawyer hideaway, replete with comfortable, stolen furniture. When young Dinny Campbell and Chris Collins determine to challenge the ghost of Andy Jim Orr, they walk into the cozy furnished room and the sudden assault of the Bear Mullan, whose chief desire, ultimately, is to tie them to posts in the barn and "give them a lick of paint," a fitting punishment for invading his privacy. But from this encounter emerges another observation on the value of recognizable evil: the Bear provides a convenient measure of courage, a test and a challenge for young manhood who oppose him. In this instance, little thirteen-year-old Chris Collins establishes himself in the world of youthful contention when he fights back, "a whirl of flying boots and hard little fists." Although saved at this time by the intervention of Joe Keenan, Chris and Dinny Campbell encounter the Bear on a snow-covered hillside where the Bear takes the small boys' sleigh away from them. The Bear's fighting is unfair; his vocabulary, filthy. Suffering defeat at the hands of Pat Rafferty, he runs "sobbing and cursing" down the hill; and, when he slips and falls, the crowd cheers the fall of the beaten tyrant.

His final defeat begins in unrest with the returning green of springtime, in association with foul-tongued army reservists who leave greasy lines on the wall they lean against [5] and who occupy themselves with telling greasy stories, spitting, smoking, and cursing. The defeat begins in resentment that, though Joe Keenan is welcomed for his music, nobody pays attention to the Bear; his superior skill in spitting into the middle of the street yields little satisfaction. The defeat occurs after the traditional chase, a chase growing out of community awareness of an attack on Lizzy the housemaid and almost simultaneously the disappearance of Gerry Campbell. Before verification of his guilt, the Bear flees from Pat Rafferty and Joe Keenan, his friends. At the end of the chase, the Bear presents a sorry appearance in his damaged new suit, and a vindictiveness about the new suit appears among onlookers because, apparently, while new it represented a triumph undeserved by a tyrant. For once, though, when Joe and Pat overtake him, they pity him and appreciate him as a human being. Dimly they understand why he has tied Gerry Campbell in the barn and given him "the brush" and why he attacked Lizzie: "The girl had smiled, expecting Gerry Campbell; and then her face had hardened when she saw the Bear, and for one awful moment the outcast had rebelled against his isolation" (257).

Contrary to the town's opinion, this exchange, in view of all suffering humanity, seems unfair; a moment of sympathy is to account for a lifetime of rebellion. The chase symbolizes society's pursuit of identifiable evil; the mystery man of Lizzie's screams and the unknown assailant who approached Gerry Campbell from behind and knocked him unconscious with a board now flees that society, and all are glad he is gone.

VI *Children and Women*

The child's world of Kiely's novels and short stories means freedom, adventure, innocent fun, and terror.[6] The child's activities, in this novel represented by Dinny Campbell and Chris Collins, include peering over unscalable cliffs, climbing trees, speculating on the adult character, wading in clear water to retrieve an antique sword, and exploring a haunted house to find it illegally occupied by the living. Between the dangers of the natural environment and awe of adults in person and in principle, the child tests his mental strength and stretches his taut muscles toward maturity. From adult conversations, not with him but over his head, he realizes the penalties of possessing a weapon—a remnant of British domination which made possession of weapons a crime against the state—and concludes that the sword must be wrapped in paper before it can be carried through the town. Between the imagery of adult figurative speech and the reality of physical appearance, the child attempts to reach independently some personal, reliable conviction; momentarily, he recoils from Alice Graham who, according to Aunt Aggie, would bring fire and brimstone on the town. He wonders: does brimstone smell like perfume? And in the midst of adult religious solemnity, the child conceals an irreverent cowboy story in the sleeves of his altar boy's robes. Bullied by Bear Mullan, the child learns to fight back. Both victim and beneficiary of adult use and misuse, he learns quickly that any innocent activity, such as sledding, may end both in pain from the flailing fists of the Bear and, almost simultaneously, in gratitude under the soothing hands of Pat Rafferty.

In a Harbour Green, in the characters of May Campbell, Dympna Campbell, and Alice Graham, gives three views of womanhood. May Campbell, lovely and desirable at age twenty, is clearly universal woman in the tradition of Eve, Helen of Troy, and, as D. H. Lawrence would have it, Hester Prynne. Holding herself aloof from the clumsiness in speech and manner of the common town boys, she scorns the companions of her sister Dympna but seeks the company of the notorious Alice Graham; for the challenge to life stirring in her finely molded limbs, the refined sexuality of her body dwells with a companion independence of spirit and determined freedom of choice in companions. She is drawn to Alice Graham as a sharer in the intricacies of feminine art; Alice, twice May's age and three times married and divorced, luxuriates in fine clothing, French perfume, and memories of far places—all these shared in uninhibited conversation, warmed with amber drink, with May.

May in her confusion about pregnancy by a man she does not want to marry thinks at first that she can look for comfort and advice from Alice Graham; but Alice has her own problems, complicated by the passing years, and, when consulted, begins to berate the town because it has neither the facilities nor the "civilization" of London or Glasgow. A newcomer who finds herself stifled by the atmosphere of the small town, she suffers the dislike of the townspeople, who regard her as a threat to propriety. When Alice fails to seduce Pat Rafferty and when Bernard Fiddis, whom she has artlessly pursued, arranges to marry May Campbell, she can only sell her hotel business and leave town.

Dympna Campbell, May's younger sister, represents innocence, simplicity, and stability. She walks unscathed among the town's riffraff, speaking freely and equally to chicken pluckers and football players,[7] as though certain they recognize a pure woman. She and her fiancé, Jim Collins, the football player, continue a long courtship, apparently free of sexual hazards, while waiting to earn enough money for marriage.

Altogether, four people represent four views of sex: May, willingness; Dympna, abstention; the Bear, rape; and Rafferty, innocence.

VII   *The Complete Picture*

Among the town's reliable and virtuous citizens, Pat Rafferty most consistently fulfills the traditional role of hero. Big of heart and stature, he intuitively knows whom to defend and whom to condemn; he takes care of Old Maxwell like a father caring for an erring child; he shames the Bear Mullan in an open fight; he can be counted on to do the "right thing." Through innocence and frustration, he misuses the power of sex; but, because he too perfectly exemplifies the town's most cherished "virtues," May in carrying his child turns away from him. She can see in marriage to him only a continuation of the routine, insular life she hates.

John Maxwell has felt the desperation of a woman both childless and friendless, confined to the rural area, to loneliness and drudgery. His wife, who blamed him for her misery, had taunted him day and night—finally, she had taunted him with a halter in her hand until he grasped one end and accomplished the death for which she had pleaded. This same motif of the rural woman driven by loneliness and monotony into mental stress affects the course of the novel *Honey Seems Bitter.*[8]

Aunt Aggie epitomizes the warped ideals of the narrow, provincial viewpoint. Ugly and virginal, she causes May to wonder sarcastically what self-sacrifice means in Aggie's caring for her brother's family when, obviously, her rigid demeanor would have frightened away any prospective lover. Above all, Aunt Aggie has remained intolerably *righteous;* her paralyzing stroke comes, therefore, as a blessing to those she has loved but always severely chastised by constantly importuning them against all "sinful" pleasure.

That the three robbers go unpunished can best be explained by Fiddis' regard for one of them—the brother of his wife. Fiddis himself becomes the target of low caricature at election time when an improvised drama by some of the town's lesser wits shows more of their ignorance and poor taste than of Fiddis' perfidy. To remain in this crowd, one must stand among them but not of them.

Finally, attitudes toward conservation and the will of God reveal themselves through the senior Rafferty's agitation for flood control. The would-be rescuers encounter "Paddy-Go-Easy," [9] as Fiddis observes, all over again: "I'll drown decent in me bed, Pat boy." And the effects of the flood demonstrate the reasons Rafferty gets little support for flood control from the people; they do indeed survive, as they have survived before.

VIII *A Look Backward and Forward*

In the "Long After O'Neill" article, Kiely told about an experience in Pomeroy when an elderly woman conducted him through her house, candle in hand, pointing out as the light fell on photograph after photograph covering the walls, all the faces of the town's football players. In *In a Harbour Green,* the mother of Brass MacManus performs this action for the visitors, Pat Rafferty and the Campbell sisters. For this and numerous other small personal strands, *In a Harbour Green* remains Kiely's favorite novel. The chicken factory, the garrisoned army, the flooding river, football on the town green—all belong to Omagh. Like other novelists who have written about their home towns, Kiely also, upon the publication of this one, encountered problems with people who thought they recognized themselves in the purely fictional episodes. He remembers a number of lawyers named Fiddis, for example; and one not named Fiddis who had "had to" marry a girl.

In relationship to the earlier novel, *Land Without Stars,* this novel continues the misuse of power as *leitmotif* and establishes two characteristics of Kiely's writing: the boys' world viewed as one of freedom, adventure, innocent fun, and terror; and sex for women, even premarital sex, viewed as natural fulfillment.[10]

CHAPTER 6

Fatalism: Call for a Miracle

Ye shall call for a miracle, taking Christ at his word.
And for this I will answer, O people, answer here and hereafter,
O people that I have loved shall we not answer together?
Padraic Pearse, "The Fool"

THE moral of *Call for a Miracle* evolves from the actions of
a God-fearing woman who considers it her "duty" to inform
a mother of what has been whispered about a prospective daugh-
ter-in-law's past. Both with and without substance, vague rumors
of personal freedom reflect typical prejudice and intolerance
against a woman whose greatest sin is independence; but, as a
result of the report to the mother, the invalid son destroys himself
in a herculean effort to reach the girl; and the girl, now deprived
of him as her only reason for existence, commits suicide. "She
was so good," weeps a friend. Before the two deaths, the miracle,
as a divinely oriented cure for physical illness, does not occur, but
another miracle exists: a growing love capable of rehabilitating
physically and spiritually both the invalid and the girl. The
mother who calls for a miracle is the one who aborts the miracle
of love.

I *The Historical Backgrounds*

The Dublin setting during World War II and a suicide plot
of the type which makes newspaper headlines enable Kiely to
use several kinds of autobiographical materials. The spinal ailment
of Dave Murray, the son, was, with slight variation, a real experience for Kiely.[1] Philomena Kane, the girl of the plot, is this
novel's tie with Kiely's homeland; she has come from North Ireland to project rough provincial honesty and near destitution; she

has a sharp eye to measure another's income by the quality of his clothing and furniture. The variety of Kiely's journalistic experience, where individuality makes a story and commonalty provides human interest, aids the variety of characters presented who have loneliness in common. Mobility, the trademark of the newspaperman, gives Brian Flood and Big Magee, characters in the novel, access to priests, policemen, and politicians. All their endeavor in *Call for a Miracle,* however, leads to the conclusion that, for a newspaperman, the stories not told are the best stories. Big Magee, modeled on an actual journalist friend of Kiely's, suppresses the desire to send to the London papers a dramatic story, in the novel, of Father Peter, the miracle worker, which he consoles himself with composing in his mind. He and Brian Flood together suppress the story of Dave Murray's death and Mary Fergus' suicide. Another autobiographical experience Kiely uses is the trip of Brian Flood to speak to a literary society. Throughout the novel, Brian Flood's separation from his wife and daughter tortures him with memories, vain hope, and despair. Reflecting on the near ostracism following the disruption of holy matrimony, Brian speaks the Kiely dictum that "marriage still means something in Ireland. There isn't any divorce."

Kiely again, in *Call for a Miracle,* uses a variation of the frame technique already established in *Land Without Stars* and *In a Harbour Green,* except that in this novel it purposefully provides an easy transition from the first-person narration to the third and gives the flavor of personal narration to the omniscient point of view. Brian Flood, the "I" of Chapter I, tells the story of Mary's death to Philomena Kane and her husband Dinny, who had left Dublin for a honeymoon shortly after Dave Murray's death and before Mary's. This setting of the stage also establishes the theme of loneliness. The novel begins with the sorrow of looking for a familiar face among a crowd of strangers; "Big Magee wasn't on the train" is the first sentence. As Brian Flood searches for companionship, remarking, "I'm a lonely man," he turns apologetic for his sentimentalism about the historic post office,[2] and the despairing tone of the novel is set by preparation to tell a story about people "all on the same level of insignificance." Brian Flood is past the age of dreaming of "success," past the age of optimism.

Because of the need to explain Mary's death to Philomena and

Dinny, the returned honeymooners, Kiely begins Chapter II approximately a year earlier with the meeting of Mary Fergus and Philomena Kane near the statue of Cuchulain in the General Post Office. Told chronologically from this point on, the story is essentially that of Mary Fergus and Brian Flood, who is in a pivotal though minor position as friend and acquaintance of all persons involved. The plot proceeds to Big Magee's recalling after Dave Murray's death both Brian Flood and Mary Fergus as they travel across Ireland to a vacation in Kerry. The final chapter (X) returns to first-person narration, an extended denouement relative to the effects of this particular tragedy and the impossibility of miracles. After all is told, Brian Flood, the separated husband, surveys the past and future and, helpless, decides not to attempt to change any of the circumstances of his own life. For him, his own particular miracle would be the "power to speak healing words to the woman living with her secret and mine, her child and mine. . . ." [3] The pity of having lost so much, of being utterly alone, describes the position of each person; in contrast the rarity of agreement, sympathy, and shared experience would make a miracle. In despair, he sees himself and others as puppets, not in the hands of God, but pulled by circumstances to react individually and not having the foresight or the strength to prevent tragedy. In fact, God is so remote that only the idea of God remains to torture. Brian's view is as black as Nathaniel Hawthorne's Young Goodman Brown's was after he returned from the forest or as that of a Samuel Beckett character who stares through the windscreen into the void. To believe that there is Someone to move the strings would be a miracle.

Throughout the novel, the home of Mrs. Murray, Pyramid Hall, symbolizes austerity and decay—of architecture and of old families. It stands among other great houses deserted by the gentry and now occupied by holy people operating nursing homes for the sick and aged; Mrs. Murray's cold, almost offensive manner complements the austerity of the lives of nuns and priests, a reduction to bitter absurdity of the custom and ceremony of the aristocracy which was prized by Yeats.[4] The pyramid, built above the house to give work to the poor in the time of famine, remains as ugly as the misery which occasioned its building, and it evokes memories of the big houses and the poor people from a century earlier as recorded in the pages of William Carleton.[5] Everything about the architecture of the place negates hope for the invalid's recovery. What Mrs. Murray's money can do to build a sunporch and to provide private nurses amounts to puny effort against a monstrosity of historic ugliness.

The post office as "the center of Ireland" dates from the 1916 rebellion and has both actual and symbolic significance. It brings together aristocratic Mary Fergus and the servant Philomena Kane. It recalls the stirring voice of the young poet Padraic Pearse who led youthful rebels into the building and who became known best for his calling for the miracle of Ireland Gaelic and Ireland free and whose people since his death—and the Partition—have never as one nation politically answered together. The narrator's thought about the futility of Pearse's hope—and, by extension, of all living together in love and understanding—comes like the expression of a last lingering regret for the Nationalistic fervor of *Land Without Stars*.

II *People That Should Have Been Loved: The Family Crisis*

With Philomena Kane as the only exception, a family crisis of some sort affects each of the characters in *Call for a Miracle*. Mrs. Murray dominates her son in the same way she had dominated his father; Dave, visualizing his father, sees him cowering in silence before the onslaught of her determination. One of Dave's nurses, who speaks of the mother as "The main trouble in this house," adds that "She bossed the father out of the house and into his grave. She bosses the son because he's tied down and can't escape." (81). Toward her son, protection of her own interests in his childhood had made her tender; but her philosophy that all men needed bossing, that all men are weak, made her terrifying. Dave, returned to his home after nearly twelve months in the hospital, recognizes his reversal to childish helplessness; and, in the tight enclosure of frame and bedclothes, he experiences something akin to a psychological return to the womb. But the symbol only half operates in a kind of duality of mind; he retains memories of himself, like Yeats's Robert Gregory, as soldier, scholar, and horseman. After a university education, while in the British army in London, a fall from a horse caused a spinal injury. Now, his mother says, "A sick man is a child again" and buys him cowboy records to inspire him to manhood. He feels the powerlessness of a child, and he sees her again as large and looming above him: "The straps and the jacket were the fingers of the unnamed terror grasping him, holding him to watch against his will the terrible symbol, a tall silhouette against a sky out of which light leaked, drop by drop, like blood from a wound or matter from an abscess, drop by drop" (31).

Mrs. Murray, almost inexplicably drawn to the strange, dark girl, Mary Fergus, shares with Mary a tendency to generalize about men. To Mrs. Murray, men are despicable for their weakness; to Mary, men are despicable for their cruelty. The one expects, the other desires, to see men in subjugation. Mary, when she first looks down on Dave in his bed of pain, sees him "broken as a man should be broken"; and her first feelings of pity, alien to her experience, come as a surprise to her. Her hatred of men was developed during her childhood when she saw her mother beaten by her father; as a result, she steals from a kind old jeweler, not because she needs rings, but because she needs to even the score against men. Called by Richard Harrity of the *New York Herald Tribune* a "Circe in modern dress," [6] she is known to the police as "I Work Alone." She has in the past accepted a fat, married man's attentions to extort money for his love letters—again, not for the money, but to make him feel foolish. Early in the novel, she explains for Philomena her attitude toward men: "They're all the same. They're all hateful. Good citizens, turning the latch-key and beating the wife. I saw it" (41).

How much sin Mary commits remains a mystery, but her individuality makes others suspect her of a great deal. The town gossips, of whom Mrs. McCarthy is a prime example, dislike a person who walks alone, seems to be unemployed but wealthy, and seems entirely indifferent to their scrutiny. The accusations Joan McCarthy makes against Mary include mostly these vagaries plus an account of following Mary one evening when Mary walked mysteriously from church to church, sitting in each one for only a few minutes; but this inordinate behavior, demonstrative of her alienation from the faithful, incriminates her. Mary is experienced enough to tease Brian Flood about his refusal to enter her bedroom; and, just after her betrayal by Joan and before Dave's death, she agrees to go to a vacation cottage in Kerry with Brian Flood. She regards him as one exception to the hatefulness of men in general. He thinks independently, and, having met her when first separated from his wife, has referred to her as "the dark night of the soul." The characterization of her "blackness" remains consistent throughout: she feels at home in storm; she commits suicide at night in the black greasy water of the Liffey. Brian was drawn to her as to a kindred spirit, perhaps because his married life had made him as unhappy and as faithless as she.

Actually, Brian Flood at age thirty-eight manages all his affairs well except his family ones, for he had married the one person with whom he could not get along. Agreeing for once with his wife about legal separation, he has become a visiting "Mr. Jones" to his daughter; and the mother usually sends the daughter away when she anticipates his surreptitious appearances; or, if she wishes to avoid him, she visits a neighbor and the daughter remains at home. During one such visit, Brian tries vainly to stuff straw into the torn body of his daughter's doll and listens to the little girl telling about her mother's tears in the night and a dream about her father's sitting on a fat woman's chair. He returns to Dublin in sorrow, knowing he cannot heal the wound in his daughter's life nor again occupy his wife's home.

Christine, the woman whom Brian almost loves, is a beautiful, seductive spinster of forty-two who had once loved the wrong man. She lives the quiet life of a Dublin working girl, temporarily yields to the temptation of a vacation with Brian Flood, but at the last minute, after a conversation with Father Peter, she runs away to a cheerless solitary life in the home town. Of her problem, Kiely writes, "In Ireland the good girl could marry respectably or quietly enter the convent or stay in the world, living modestly and chastely all the days of her life. But the beautiful girl could not be so readily accommodated; for small places and small people can accept goodness or badness, while they are only puzzled by beauty" (67). In the end, Christine proves to be a combination of both virtues—beauty and goodness—and quietly accepts both kinds of problems.

Philomena Kane alone has in her background a desirable home life and makes a successful marriage. The forthright honesty of her provincial father guides her in all her dealings. She conjures his face, "square like her own, but rough and red and perspiring from hot bending in the sun-clamping turf" and realizes, though he had never been in a city, the accuracy of his predictions of evil to be encountered there. Not pure and simple and easily identified as at home, a thief in Dublin "could be a well-dressed girl as lovely as a film actress." A Dublin hospital maid, employed by Mary Fergus, Philomena always wears red and valiantly defends the chastity her clothing does not symbolize. After a primitive zoo scene, with all the earthiness of her escort's honest humor, she chooses him, a "Dublin jackeen," for her husband and becomes the envy of all the other heartbroken people who would seek in marriage the blessing of peace.

III *"Shall We Not Answer Together": The Religious Disputes*

The problem with a physical cure for Dave Murray as a miracle, if one could occur, is that its mere contemplation involves people in religious politics. Mrs. Murray's fear of being converted to Catholicism makes her hesitant about writing to Father Peter. Mrs. McCarthy, who has introduced the subject of Father Peter's faith healing, would score a personal triumph against her girlhood "friend" Mrs. Murray if a cure for Dave proved Catholicism the only answer to life's many dilemmas. Mrs. Murray confides to Mary, "Then if you're not a Catholic they want to convert you," shortly before Mrs. McCarthy writes to Father Peter, "Maybe the poor boy's recovery would help his mother to see the true light." With one mother secretly distrustful, hoping the miracle will not occur to cast doubt on her religious position and to prevent her proving her strength in curing him herself, and with the other mother openly aggressive, hoping for the miracle to strengthen her own Catholic arguments, the prayers of Father Peter can scarcely rise through the atmosphere of contention. Ironically, at the moment Father Peter lays his hands on Dave Murray's head and prays, Mrs. McCarthy burns with impatience to give Mrs. Murray the information which will destroy her son; Dave welcomes the sign that the tiresome interview will soon be over; Mrs. Murray regards the priest as "neither sinister nor repulsive, just insignificant."

Mrs. McCarthy, eager and aggressive in doing good, keeps up appearances with embroidering vestments for the clergy in Africa and with referring often to her other daughter, a nun. She feels uncomfortable in the presence of Evelyn Murray but considers it her Christian duty to continue the friendship, though it lacks sincerity. When she relaxes "from piosity into the uncharity more natural to her tedious nervousness," she speaks of Mrs. Murray's treatment of Dave as cruelty to animals. Somewhat ashamed of her plump daughter Joan's bouncing vitality, she suffers horrible embarrassment and anger when Joan returns drunk from a hike where for the first time she had enjoyed the companionship of a young man. Slapping Joan's face, screaming her horror, and citing Mary Fergus as an example of decorum, Mrs. McCarthy forces Joan, who has long been jealous of Mary, to answer the charges by telling what Joan has just learned of Mary's past—the mystery of her source of income and her solitude. Having lost Dave's attention in the past, Joan now scores twice in releasing two kinds of pent-up hatreds and gives Mrs. McCarthy the ammunition she needs against her friend. At the earliest possible moment, Mrs. McCarthy hastens to tell Mrs. Murray, "You have allowed a viper to enter your house."

But no one ever learns from tragedy; no one ever sees his part in it as a fault. Brian Flood, reflecting on past events, thinks "May McCarthy and her daughter Joan will remember nothing for they have no place among the people with memories. Evelyn Murray will remember everything but in the way of the dark people whose memories are shut against the world because the memory is part of the guarded soul" (285). Father Peter, in anxious self-awareness that he is prying into Mary Fergus' affairs, alludes to himself in reciting a childish rhyme which more accurately identifies Mrs. McCarthy's kind of piety: "It is a splendid thing to be with the saints in glory/ But to meet the saints on earth is a hell of another story."

The most successful characterization in the story is that of Father Peter. Unimpressive in appearance and painfully nearsighted, he claims his vocation is chicken farming; and Big Magee, looking for a story, fails utterly to confirm what might be merely rumor of Father Peter's miraculous healing powers. When speaking of peace to end the war, the priest makes a kind of futuristic analysis of the Dave Murray tragedy: "We all stand around expecting a miracle, and it doesn't happen because we haven't really asked God for a miracle." No one really asks God for a miracle to cure Dave.

The priest is the one person in the novel who loves everyone he meets,[7] and he succeeds in winning Dave's reluctant admiration. Responding to Dave's comment that he does not know how to pray, Father Peter asks, "Who does? Who does?" A short time later he discovers in the silent, morose Mary Fergus a sense of humor and succeeds in making her laugh outright. He speaks to her of the loss which must accompany any gain as a favor from God, and he mentions the losses of the criminal nailed to the cross, who was left with only "his mother and a young fellow and a poor girl that the people were talking about" for friends. Father Peter's message that "there are always a few people who share the sorrow of our loss" should have special restorative significance for Mary who has lost so much, and she takes him to her home and gives him a much-appreciated melodeon. Big Magee's silent composing of a news story he will never send to the London papers ends dramatically with a comment on the character of the man: "And bidding farewell to this man of mystery and miracle I said to myself—God has visited his people" (258). Father Peter's people are, sincerely, *all* people.

Father Peter, by all conventional social standards, must be the most lonely of all the characters who function independently. The difference is his failure to recognize his loneliness because of his concern for "the suffering of the whole world, man nailed to the Cross and never knowing that he shared the enviable fate of the Son of God." He succeeds in making Mary forget her bitterness and in having Christine remember her morals. Quoting Cardinal Newman, "Never less alone than when alone," Father Peter teaches without preaching, simply by living his faith and by making bright conversation, interspersed with much laughter.

As Brian's epithet for her, "the dark night of the soul," indicates, Mary Fergus has no religion; though she once attends church with Philomena and also kneels with Philomena to receive Father Peter's blessing, she performs these acts as social amenities rather than as religious duties. Dave, for his part, addresses Father Peter as "Sir," a formality which always marks an uncomfortable Protestant. In the end, Dave emerges from his tomblike encasement, sardonically pronouncing to an empty house, "Lazarus, come forth." Philomena, as the only person who finds love, is also the only person whose faith is pure and simple, and secure.

IV *The Lost Love Motif and Miracles*

In addition to Brian Flood's separation from his wife and daughter, Christine has only memories of a former love, a man who was destined to marry no one and on whom she wasted the "best" years. Now reunited in Dublin with Brian, a childhood sweetheart, she shares with him the experiences of futility and the collapse of worn-out dreams. Recognizing that Brian will never be free, she agrees temporarily to become his paramour; but, on a shopping trip with Father Peter, she listens to Father Peter's analysis of Saint Paul's statement, "It is better to marry than to burn." Saint Paul, said Father Peter, "was talking to men. Women never need so much persuasion." On the loneliness theme, Father Peter touches her soul when he remarks, "The good can afford to be lonely. Or maybe it's the strong can afford to be lonely" (257). Reflecting on human tendencies to display faults on all sides, Christine determines her fault will not be a sexual sin and flees, just minutes before the expected Brian arrives to find, not a lovely woman waiting for his arms, but a hastily scrawled note confessing her cowardice—and her determination.

Dave Murray also has loved a German girl who loved another man; and the sorrow of his lost love, especially as he pictures her among bombed ruins, drains him of a will to live and retards his recovery. Of the remaining characters, Big Magee the journalist and Frank Fox the policeman have no loves except their work, nor, apparently, do they need any; Big Magee sees people as newspaper stories, and Frank Fox sees them as case histories.

The stark nudity of loneliness makes the characters of *Call for a Miracle* stand out from the blurred crowds of Dublin. Except for the romance of Philomena and Dinny, the gaiety of much dining and drinking in pubs and of even an excursion into the country for a literary meeting has an air of contrivance, as if it were necessary to manufacture happiness. All the characters widowed, separated, or unattached would be suspicious if the accident of sincere happiness were ever to occur. Perhaps the fault lies in an inability to fix wrong as other than pervasive: Mrs. McCarthy views wrong as any shortness of Catholic conviction; Mrs. Murray, as any type of weakness; Dave, as physical confinement; Mary, as the male half of humanity; and Brian, as a single error in choice of a mate. Though Brian alone blames only himself, he remains totally uncritical of the others, viewing all humanity in solitude from behind his newspaper in a crowded restaurant, and knowing that "if all went well" it would be too much to ask of any god.

From the complexity of these human situations, it is no wonder that each reviewer of *Call for a Miracle* interpreted the miracle differently. To Doran Hurley [8] of *The Capuchin Annual* the miracle comes to Philomena; she finds love. Richard Harrity [9] wrote that Kiely "has performed something of a minor miracle by taking what appears to be standard Irish parochial material and turning it into a book with universal appeal." James Kelly [10] saw that Father Peter is "unable to perform the miracle of healing but able to bring off a greater one—that of helping men and women see themselves clearly." Nash K. Burger [11] focused on Brian Flood, who has "lost his faith in miracles and . . . experiences none." Kevin Sullivan wrote that [12] "it is this loneliness . . . which calls for a miracle." Bernardine Kielty [13] looked to the hereafter: "Father Peter's miracle . . . flings the two he would most want to help to their destruction, and presumably to their God."

In the Kiely novel sequence, this book is a dark view of the world with only patches of light and leads into the novel of the next year which has a bitter title and a murder plot.

CHAPTER 7

The Jaundiced View: Honey Seems Bitter

THE plot of *Honey Seems Bitter* develops through the narration of pedantic and neurotic Donagh Hartigan, who seeks the solitude of a small town twelve miles north of Dublin to recover from a nervous breakdown. With his foil, the handsome, healthy, and prosperous George Butler, he discovers the body of Lily Morgan, strangled in her bed. Jim Walsh, lonely and ill-kempt, is accused of Lily's murder; but he refuses to defend himself and hangs for the crime, thereby permitting the gallows to serve as an instrument of suicide to avoid prolonged suffering from lung disease. Soon after the murder, George Butler introduces Donagh Hartigan to the beautiful and seductive Emily Rayel, who believes herself frigid because of an unfortunate childhood experience.

After becoming engaged to George Butler, Emily nevertheless fears his outbursts of temper and finds herself increasingly attracted to the less self-assured but also less volatile Donagh Hartigan. They escape for a weekend together, but a neighbor of Donagh, jealous of George Butler's preference for Emily, betrays their secret. A scene of lovemaking which promises a future together for Donagh and Emily is followed by a fight between George and Donagh in which George confesses the murder and Donagh leaves George wounded. Resolving to protect himself and his affair with Emily, Donagh goes to the police; but George, after Emily's refusal to leave the country with him, drives his car over a cliff. Emily, believing herself responsible for George's death, refuses to see his rival, Donagh; and Donagh returns to the city.

I *The Mind and the Sensibilities*

In the beginning of the novel, Donagh Hartigan's exaggerated awareness of physical processes—perspiration on the forehead, phlegm in the throat, heart thumping against the chest—mark him as a neurotic whose troubles, as Frank O'Connor phrased it, are certainly in himself. Increasing his problems, his mother sends him almost daily letters which he delays reading. Requiring her "dear boy" to return home to be properly cared for, she upbraids him for trying to recover from his illness and encourages him to imagine himself ill—so that she can nurse him. At the time, his denial of her stands as his one triumph on the road to better health.

At every turn, everyone except Donagh's mother advises him to shake himself out of himself, but the process presents un-resolvable contradictions. How, for example, does one turn his thoughts to others when much-needed companionship destroys self-reliance? The first step occurs with the discovery of suspicious-looking Jim Walsh who is in Donagh's home without permission, and Donagh detains him by slamming the door, proud of the "decisive speed" of this one action. With pitiful Jim Walsh, he discovers his appetite; and, with George Butler as new-found friend to introduce him to society and his share in the discovery of the murder to give him community status, he tends to notice less the continued superiority of Butler and the undeserved neglect of the community. Gradually, Donagh loses his tendency to quote poetry at inopportune moments to uncomprehending companions; and, as he becomes more active in society, particularly with Emily Rayel, his beloved books of Blaise Pascal, Giovanni Papini, Jean Paul Sartre, Fëdor Dostoevski, Epictetus, and Sir Thomas Malory, consume less and less of his time. The tendency to intellectualize human activities as if they were poems or novels continues, however; Hartigan's esthetic distancing at the trial brings swift condemnation from George Butler, who exclaims, "You enjoy this, Harty, you microbe. . . . Where's your pity? That bastard in the dock? That girl on the bed?"

When Hartigan meets George Butler's "unofficial" fiancée, Emily Rayel, he cannot screen from his mind the lines of the fourteenth-century Provençal poet Eustache Deschamps who wrote of beauty and firm busts seated high. Deschamps' line which Donagh applies to Emily, "Sui-je, sui-je, sui-je belle?" recurs as a *leitmotif*; and the *leitmotif* must always be a question, for Emily herself has no knowledge of the uses of beauty.

Donagh detects a childish lisp in Emily's voice and describes her innocent eyes as those of a child. Watching her closely, he regards her as some quaint thing found between the pages of an old book, quickly guesses from her diffident handling of George Butler that she must be "religious or frigid or innocent or ignorant or just afraid,"[1] and later observes the oddly abstracted way she stares at Butler's hand which is cupped over her heart. When George drunkenly falls asleep, she praises the company of a quiet man—Donagh—and soon, having gone to Donagh's hut to dry her feet, confesses to abnormality. At the age of nine, she says, a strange man had led her up a sidestreet, where nothing really happened, but the attitude of her parents afterward had caused her "who could stir desire in a stock or a stone" to remain as "cold and unmoved as a marble pillar in a cathedral vault." She knows that he, being neurotic, will understand; he rejoices in having found someone like himself.

Secretly, Emily and Donagh meet in a greenhouse where the exotic flowers create an unreal setting and mark the turning point—for Donagh, betrayal of the friend, George Butler; for Emily, a gradual relaxing of her coldness. From this point, it becomes easier for Donagh to rationalize the betrayal of friendship and for Emily to learn love. Eventually, he tells himself Butler "had so much and I so little," and Emily responds with a cry of pain on a fairy hill[2] and late that night lies awake in her hotel room until Donagh enters. The air of unreality surrounding greenhouse and fairy-hill romance acts as foreshadowing for Donagh's ultimate realization that he has not won Emily's love. Later, Butler bitterly denounces Hartigan for this betrayal of friendship: "Harty, you were my friend and you did that to me. I've done murder for what you stole from me" (162).

In Emily, George Butler has affianced the most beautiful and the most wealthy girl in town; but Butler wins the liking of everyone, whatever the relationship to him as servant, companion, friend, or aspiring wife. Though well educated and a journalist, at a local bar he adopts colloquial speech to make the slattern attendant his slave: "Aye, God help us, the world's full of trouble," he sympathizes with her horror of the murder. He is a splendid, generous host; and at his hotel he confidently violates the residents' rules with the explanation, "In this place, they eat out of my hands." He knows Dublin well enough to recognize a kip (brothel) from a street address—the place where the accused murderer Jim Walsh was arrested—and proceeds to describe with firsthand knowledge the "native Irish bordello. Fleas, disease, and fights in the back yard." Since everybody is glad to know Butler, he plays the field, including in his magazine column much tongue-in-cheek praise of bad theatrical performances with the rationalization, "Don't they all love me? Amn't I everybody's friend?"

But George Butler refuses to commit himself to love for Emily. He confides to Donagh his past failures. "My general rule of life," he says, "is drink until I want a lay and take it if it's handy, and if it's not handy drink more and forget about it." At the same time, he admits that Emily is an exception; she "registers in the soul" (55–56). When George's bad temper first manifests itself in dangerous driving, Donagh begins to understand why Emily fears him. Next, on very slight provocation, Butler fells with one blow a poor inoffensive fellow in a bar. But George continues to excel; he wins at the races when everyone else loses; and, at a drunken party when others become ill, he remains organized, directed, and controlled. His remark at his first meeting with Hartigan one blissful August morning, "God, this is peace. It should never be broken," does not appear ironic until months later when Donagh learns that George had just a few hours earlier murdered Lily Morgan.

Donagh envies George's ability to joke on the telephone a few minutes after discovery of Lily Morgan's body: "Got mixed up in a murder. Yes. Murder. Really and truly. No. Not my own. Not yet, anyway. . . . Good-bye dear. See you on the gallows" (14).

George's success, based on poise and self-command, stems from adaptability and versatility. But this same adaptability and versatility, stretched to duplicity, make an apparently fine fellow a murderer; Lily Morgan had become too serious, and he needed no other motive. Later, he plans to kill Donagh Hartigan for having slept with Emily Rayel. He becomes violent when anyone takes the direction of the action out of his hands. With the range of his ability, it becomes questionable where the real man is; but such range, ironically, assures him social success. Donagh Hartigan, on the other hand, is sincerely pedantic when the quotations crowding his mind leap to his lips—but his sincerity makes him a social failure. In the end, when the question about whether or not Emily loves George Butler seems to be answered positively by her inconsolable guilt about his death, George triumphs even after death; by the manner of his death, he has outwitted both Donagh and the police. Donagh thinks, "How splendid to be dead and pitied and to die by drowning rather than by the merited rope." Of his affair with Emily, Donagh realizes the fear that blasts all pride in conquest: in sharing Emily's bed, he was only a George Butler surrogate.

II And Things Are Not What They Seem

Before Donagh Hartigan discovered Lily Morgan's body, he had met her at the rest home where "the company can be very exhausting." Donagh accepts these little ironies, but no amount of experience prepares him for the inaccuracies of his best deductions. Approaching Lily Morgan's cottage for the first time, he sees it, complete with rose-covered white walls, as a "page from an E. V. Lucas essay on seed merchants' catalogues"; and he imagines it as the perfect place for a widow and her "virtuous simpering daughter who might know about sorrow but not about sin and certainly not about screams" (8). A few months later, he finds flower stalks rotting and whitewashed stones blemished. His own illusions about another man's daughter shattered, he listens to this same widow destroy another of his theories: "But it's a sinful world, Mr. Hartigan. It's little any of us knows of the wickedness the devil puts into the heart of man" (193). At this time, also, the widow unknowingly contradicts her testimony given at the trial of Jim Walsh. Formerly, she had sworn Lily had never mentioned another man; now she tells Donagh how many times her daughter had spoken of Donagh.

The description of Jim Walsh, a man with lung disease and a shady past who arrived like a derelict newly washed up on the coast, evokes memories of Charles Dickens' Magwitch in *Great Expectations*. But Kiely, when questioned about a possible connection, answered that there was none. The original Jim Walsh was casually met in a bar where migratory Irish navvies and agricultural laborers from counties Mayo and Galway assembled. The original was much as described in the novel: "a fine shape of a man gone to seed, and with tuberculosis." He wore a long coat and had deserted the Irish Guards. A message he asked Kiely to deliver to a relative in Dublin was "coldly received." [3]

The fictional Jim Walsh, who looks like a criminal, has returned from England penniless and saddened by the preference of his former fiancée, Lily Morgan, for George Butler. Known to the villagers as a "horse-jockey," a man of no certain occupation, he attributes the collapse of one lung and the deterioration of the other to too many nights sleeping in ditches. He has stolen the whiskey he carries and has received the mincemeat (hamburger) as charity, both of which he shares for warmth of fireside and companionship with the recuperating Donagh Hartigan; and, entirely foreign to his appearance, he professes an appreciation of the poet Rainer Maria Rilke. He mentions doing a favor the night before for Mrs. Kavanagh in the next hut; and, before he departs and while Donagh sleeps soundly, he straightens and tidies the house and washes the dishes.

The next time Donagh sees him at the deposition, Walsh makes no effort to presume on friendship, nor does he defend himself at the trial. For Donagh, the sight of three, white, wild swallows on the shield-shaped label of a whiskey bottle will forever bring memories of Jim Walsh. At this time, the soul of Lily Morgan has already flown; he will recall at the hour of Jim Walsh's execution the ancient custom of kneeling "to pray for the safe journeying of whatever it was went out over their heads like a bird"; and the third death will be that of George Butler. Executed for a crime he did not commit, Jim Walsh has the purity of intention and the stainlessness of soul adequately symbolized by the white wild swallows.

The next-door neighbor, Mrs. Kavanagh, stirs Donagh's desires and imagination when he observes in her plump body, he thinks, the makings of a desirable marriage. He envies her husband's return after a day's work to "rest and steak and other things," and he torments himself during the long nights with a desire to listen at the thin walls of the cottage to the creaking of a single bunk. Later, when he sees the Kavanagh's small hut lined with sacred pictures and observes their separate bunks, he learns also of the husband's prayer rituals with his mother. Mrs. Kavanagh appears a sloven, identifies her husband as a "saint" and "monk"; instead of the love marriage hopefully imagined by Donagh, she tells a long story of her rejection by Jim Walsh for Lily Morgan and of her subsequent determination to marry for spite any other available man. Donagh, who hears in Mr. Kavanagh's voice the hoarseness of hatred at mention of Jim Walsh, turns to see misery in the man's eyes.

Though Mr. Kavanagh eventually succeeds in his marriage and resolves Donagh's early errors about it, Donagh never resolves a confusion about the two women, Emily Rayel and Lily Morgan. Lily's illness and Emily's frigidity, having fragile similarity to his neuroticism, had drawn both women imaginatively to him. His dreams of romance with Lily, after her murder, were transferred to Emily. Emily's voice, "level and gentle and unhurried," at first startles him with its similarity to Lily's. At the deposition, when the sight of Mrs. Morgan's face reminds him of Lily, he transfers his thoughts to recollection of Emily's face; later Emily's account of the hypnotist who stopped his heart brings to Donagh the memory of George Butler bending to feel the cold breast of Lily Morgan, and a vision of Lily's face reminds him that, because of her death, he came to Emily Rayel. Finally, he sees a parallel between the hands which closed over Lily's throat and those which untied Emily's childhood hair ribbon; both were *crimes passionnels*.

The confusion continues until the very end when Donagh realizes that Emily does not love him and he plays the game of imagining their experiences with him reversed: "Lily lay on the ancient forth in the sunny whin-sheltered corner. Emily on a bed screamed before strangling hands" (194). That he should regard such as a "pleasantly imaginative swapping game" proves him not far removed from the viciousness which he had deplored in George Butler; indeed, the uncharacteristic depths of violence revealed in Donagh's personality during the fight scene constitute another of those unpredictable reverses. As a child, he remembers, "a fight for me had always meant standing in one place as if my feet were screwed to the ground, closing my eyes, flailing emptiness with my fists, hoping that I'd hit something and yet afraid to augment my opponent's anger" (158). When he realizes Butler means to kill him, he does not stop to consider the justice of the armed against the unarmed; Donagh, who flails a heavy pine bludgeon in a blood-red mist of anger, becomes as inhuman as the murderer he assails.

In the midst of many things which are not what they seem, neither is Donagh the person he appears to be. The crowning disappointment of Emily's rejection brings him to the certainty of uncertainty; "There was nothing reliable in the world, nothing steady, nothing competently known," he reflects. A person with nerves seeking something permanent must realize the permanence of impermanence. Perhaps this realization is what the healthy people without nerves have always known.

III *The Sweets of Life Turned Sour*

Though the plot of *Honey Seems Bitter* is a straightforward love-triangle murder mystery with none of the irrelevancies for which some reviewers criticized *Call for a Miracle,* the theme is the betrayal of friendship—a theme developed skillfully through Naturalistic details which support the suspicion that, though the sun now shines like honey or yellow wine spilling through woodland bowers, it will soon look different. The Naturalistic details accumulate through a variety of settings. In a local pub, "A slattern of woman chewing the bacon rinds of a late breakfast poured our whiskies" (15). In the greenhouse of Hartigan's first secret meeting with Emily, "the ranks of begonias smelled unwholesomely like unwashed old ladies crouched close to radiators in the corners of crowded churches" (83). Passing through a village on the way to the races, Donagh observes "Discarded tins and cabbages and chamber-pots half embedded in mud" (119).

The Irish reviewers did not so much object to such unflattering descriptions as they did to the behavior of the characters: murder in a quiet village, seduction of an innocent girl, continual drinking in pubs. These activities, they tritely hoped (as they have since the days the irate Dublin citizen roared at Sean O'Casey, "There are no prostitutes in Dublin!"), would not be regarded as typically Irish. A reviewer for the *Irish Independent* [4] found blasphemous the description of a witness at the trial: "a thin, angular creature who looked like a whist-fiend and a member of many pious sodalities." Another spoke of Joycean revolt,[5] but Kiely has never rejected his Jesuit background; he has objected to narrowness and hypocrisy in religion, as in Mrs. McCarthy of *Call for a Miracle,* but not to religion itself. In short, a bit of circumstantial irony occurred with this book about betrayal of friendship; it was banned in Ireland, as if Kiely in writing it had betrayed his country. Actually, in writing uncomplimentary description and characterization, Kiely merely seeks objectivity. Not all his characters, for example, bandy the Holy Name;[6] but some of them do.

The disquieting thought about uncomplimentary description, however, is that sometimes appearances are not deceptive. Or should one say that sunshine, like honey, is more real than sunshine like jaundice, or love more real than hate? When and where is the spasmodic glint of perception which pivots the healthy to the jaundiced point of view? After the death of the betrayed friend and the loss of lovely Emily, the sunshine seems to Donagh to be yellow like jaundice. Marcus Aurelius, one of Donagh's favorite authors, had written in Verse 57 of the Sixth Meditation, "Honey tastes bitter to the jaundiced and water is horrible to a person with rabies; and a ball is a fine thing to little children. Why then am I angry with anyone? Do you think that a false opinion has less power than bile in the jaundiced or poison in one who is bitten by a mad dog?" [7]

Disregarding the bonds of friendship has turned bitter the sweets of love. Was Marcus Aurelius ignorant, or did he merely pretend ignorance, of his wife's adventures? Circumstances and the yellow wintry sunlight bring Donagh to meditations of his own: "On a fairy hill Emily and I had sipped our pot of honey. To them that are sick of the jaundice, said old Marcus, that meditative cuckold of a horse-jockey, honey seems bitter. Jaundice yellowed all things, set them shaking, so that at the bridge I could fool myself that I needed a rest" (192). A few months earlier, the rest home had proved exhausting; now a rest in a quiet village has proved exhausting. In a need for rest and a return to his mother, Donagh has come full circle. In making friends and regaining his appetite, he has learned nothing.

Bookish Donagh, in the process of moving toward betrayal of a friend and in fighting an overprotective mother, had remembered once an old Gaelic folk tale that told how the human mind can encompass the action of hours in a single fleet instant. Swearing amnesty between two warring clans, the Brennans approached the Brady cabin, where the father Brennan instructed the son to hide his knife in the thatch. Having done so, the son entered the cabin to find his father wounded and bleeding; and there followed long days of pursuit of the enemies, after which the son with the knife on his belt returned to the Brady cabin and found his father laughing and drinking with his former enemies. The unspoken moral of the old tale, as Kiely construes it, may be twofold: "perhaps an honest bare blade is better than a blade hidden in the body of a neighbour's house, or . . . a man may live a whole life of dream in the moment of stabbing and pulling the blade out again, or in the moment of strangling a girl" (116). In this context Butler's accusation that Hartigan lacked pity for Jim Walsh and Lily Morgan no longer appears hypocritical; rather, it remains consistent with his characteristic congeniality, the murder itself being one of those fleeting phenomena of the human mind.

The story has relevance to many human situations, but Donagh tries to apply it to the matter of independence of his mother. "When and where," he asks, "had been the gesture that had liberated me from my mother's house and the proximity of my sisters?" (117). In his pride at the decisiveness of this gesture, he fails to realize that his strength must come from an acceptance of, not a denial of, his mother. In spite of noble Joycean, and other, efforts, one cannot alter his past nor deny his origins. True, when the friend is betrayed and the love is lost, in a world "dying of jaundice," Donagh is able to return; but he has not reached a new plateau in his personal development. Earlier, in response to the mother's vision of his returning "sensible and glad to be home again," he had promised himself, "No, never shall sun or moon that moment see." But, at the end, his reason for returning plays him false: "I could never be a good son to her, but I'd live there for a while, endure my sisters for a while until their healthy offensiveness had helped me to forget my friend, George Butler" (193). As long as the reason for the return is an escape from another problem, there is no acceptance and no triumph in the decision to live with his mother rather than without. Hartigan returns confirmed in his neuroticism; he has never learned that "The troubles are always in ourselves" and that the solution must come from ourselves.

CHAPTER 8

Between Heaven and Hell:
The Cards of the Gambler

THE circle from antiquity to the present has functioned as more than symbol of man's relationship to others, to the round earth, to the rotating planets, or to the Oneness of Divine Will. To look, for example, at the stone circles of prehistoric Ireland and to search for symbols of spiritual and political unity in the twentieth century force reflection on the continuity of human experience. A second type of continuity of human experience emerges from the old folk tales which told of often fantastic human adventures with unspoken comment on real human problems. For such a purpose, Kiely digressed briefly from straight plot development in *Honey Seems Bitter* to tell an old Gaelic tale of a man who concealed a deadly weapon when he entered a house as a guest; [1] for the same purpose in *Cards of the Gambler* Kiely retells in a contemporary setting an old Gaelic tale about a card-playing doctor. Like the endless circle, which is the dominant symbol of this novel that is rife with ancient symbols, the twice-told tale unites past and present in a novel whose theme is the continuity of human desire.

I The Primitive Origins

A doctor, having fallen through excessive gambling into debt, disrespect, and marital difficulties, stakes his last possessions, his car and overcoat; loses; and returns home to find a third child born to his wife. On his way to ask a priest to baptize the child, he meets God and Death; God baptizes the child while Death stands sponsor, and the gambler seeks of God three wishes: success at cards; healing of the sick except when Death sits at the head of the bed; and—a wish kept secret from Death—power over anyone who sits in his car. For seven years he keeps his bargain, and his professional fame grows; but Death takes first his children's puppy, then the woman he loves, then his son. Once the doctor breaks his bargain by turning his patient's bed; once he leaps from a bus before it careens into a canal. At last indifferent, he returns to the scene of childhood innocence, teaches a tearful child a prayer, dies, and goes to purgatory and then to heaven. A prologue, seven brief italicized interludes, and an epilogue parallel the Gaelic with the novel versions.

To achieve an atmosphere of eeriness, Kiely artfully blends the real and the fantastic, the literal and the metaphoric. The desire for cards, a game which challenges the intuition rather than factual knowledge, constitutes a reaching for some supernatural power, "sets the half-conscious body and the satiated soul swinging in the air between the fear of loss and the hope of gain."[2] The inanimate cards become the flesh and blood of life, the cloth a "green field where kings and queens and jesters in two different colours, red for blood and black for death, lie on beds of red diamonds, dark trefoil, bleeding hearts, the heads of black spears" (14). Precise measured hours and minutes mingle with imaginative personification: "At twenty minutes to five the morning came into the room, a thin bit of a girl squeezing through a half-opened window, unsettling heavy clay-brown curtains, her thin body naked and wet like the cold dripping scales of a mermaid, a chill breeze of a girl who knew nothing about the sun" (5). This setting recalls for the gambler an ancient folk song: "Here we go round the mulberry bush, . . . on a cold and frosty morning," a song with seven words repeated three times and an image of circling dance. The image recurs throughout the novel at strategic moments to herald an unnatural event, as when the doctor walks into a pub where twelve men dance with joined hands, and he meets God. Sometimes the unreal is merely hinted at, as when Death enters the pub: "A door opened in the corner behind him. A man came in briskly but no light came in."

The circle is more than a metaphor drawn from historic time; it is itself timeless and therefore serves a multitude of symbolic purposes. The stone circles, which in Ireland are commonplace (one source lists 163 as the number of cromlechs in County Sligo alone),[3] were symbolic of the great orb of the sun and usually were formed of thirty stones representing the thirty days of the month. The circular dance, like the wheel as a symbol, imitated the rotary motion of the sun; and circular movement among ancient Hindus and Greeks was regarded, because of geometrical self-sufficiency, as the one perfect form of movement; and the wheel, since it must have an unmoving center, in some societies represented perfect spiritual attainment or, through self-creation and self-preservation, a harmony of all forms of being. Dancing around the circle of spiritual perfection contrives the effect of rest versus motion and of the One in the Many. God, then, may be regarded as an Unmoved Mover—the pure unmoved center of the wheel, especially because He makes His will effective without utterance or gesture. Pagan and Christian mythology blend when the sun is seen as giver of life, when God is regarded as Creator, and when both are represented by the same symbol.[4] In *The Cards of the Gambler*, the continuity of symbols from paganism to Christianity supports the theme of continuity of desire.

The stationary circle, representing the roundness of the earth or sun, and the rotary circle, representing the turning of the planets, sufficed to locate man geometrically in his relationship to the universe. At this point, the mysticism of the number seven becomes important for man's spatial orientation; he sees himself as "here" and the remaining spatial directions up, down, east, west, north, and south. Symbolic of perfect order and of the sum of the important ternary (usually concerning heavenly attributes) and of the quaternary (usually concerning earthly attributes), seven also represented the seven planets, the seven virtues, and the seven vices. When rearranged in groups of three, seven circles formed the immutable nine; the word *nine* in Hebrew was also the word for truth, especially derivative because the number nine, when multiplied, reproduces itself: two times nine equals eighteen (one plus eight equals nine).[5] There are in the novel seven gamblers: the doctor, the draper, the grocer, the university professor, the bookie, the factory owner, and the professional golfer. When the gambling doctor, confident of his superior skill at cards, near the end of his life pits his skill against an unknown man who turns up a nine after each time the doctor turns up seven, the doctor names the man God.

From the first utterance of "Here we go round the mulberry bush," the circle image appears prominently to suggest various human responsive and intuitive experiences. Returning home, the gambler-doctor regards suburban life as "the poise and swing and rhythm of an expensive dressdance." The beloved strong woman, the wife's cousin, is said, when she spoke, to make the world whirl faster. Escape, when contemplated, offers three choices: the road, the river, the rope; "and in the circle of the rope and the sinuous body of the river, hope came to an abrupt end." The gambler meditates the winding road of life ahead of his third son; he climbs the steep stairway to an upstairs pub where twelve Oriental-visaged men in mourning clothes sit in a circle. Such a dance of twelve men represents, no doubt, the twelve signs of the zodiac and hence all space and time; it introduces the contrasting thirteenth man who sits immobile, watching the "twelve men spinning like the world spinning." They break into the mulberry-bush song, and one grasps the waist of a girl and whirls her in an orgiastic reel. The mourning clothes for death and the orgiastic reel for life then bring from the thirteenth man an unneeded explanation: "A party for death and a party for birth." The meaning of the mulberry bush becomes clear when the doctor sees the twelve men as "all men circling around the tree of life"; however, in spite of calling himself damned, he does not understand until he reaches heaven that the party celebrates his metaphoric death and rebirth.

The circular image also identifies man's primitive sense of place qualities when he realizes an urge to return to places he has known not so much geographically as experientially and responsively, particularly for a state of innocence, and, therefore, joy. This state is the doctor's favorite topic: "Adam discovering the road back to Eden, the great salmon returning to the red gravel where its life began, the desire in every soul for the dark original womb" (31).

The circle means also the familiar experience of the mind that spins with imponderables so that the doctor, when Death is gone, closes his eyes with bedlam whirling around him and awakens to doubt and eerie, motionless quiet. He now sees the enduring stone cathedral of baptism as the center of concentric circles around which lie the other churches of city and country, as if Christians have unknowingly duplicated the cromlechs. The first circle includes the city churches; the second, the suburban fringes. Here the gambler-doctor walks around the last curve of the road, itself a fringe marking the threshold of his new, weird existence following a meeting with God and Death. The gambler-doctor, preparing to make his third wish, remembers his past desires "whirling like dancers before a sultan," and in the next moment the present world of his existence circles about him, spinning faces and figures and places by the thousand.

When seven years later, the doctor turns his patient's bed to defy death, his eyes light on circular windows, and he reflects that nothing he can do will weaken the steel spring of the soul of the young Spanish woman who rejects a hated love in spite of danger to herself. Later, leaping from the bus in an unexpected secluded field, he confronts a group of twenty singing and dancing persons and obtains from them portentous directions. To return to town (the origin of his journey and, allegorically, the origin of the soul's journey, heaven) he must fly; but, humorously, the method of actual flight is the *téléferique*. Finally, he confesses to Death his desire for one thing more—to return to innocence, to the moment of pure faith; and, when he returns to the scene of his one childhood happiness, he "completes the circle" of his days.

The circle, then, binds the gambler-doctor to physical qualities of the spinning earth. When associated with God, the circle describes the spirit and the universe. God, leaving the pub, gestures with a hand "circling as the room was circling," from the gambler's viewpoint, and his voice is "a golden winged bird circling against the circling of the room." God, leaving the baptism before granting the three omnipotent wishes, travels with uncanny speed to a mountain and stands looking at ancient symbols of immutability and immortality, a "mystic circle of green revolving around a center of ancient grey stones and a crooked mountain ash" (59). No pagan-Christian polarity exists here; whatever this God is known by, He remains immutable.

Death, that other ineluctable being, sees all of life as anything but a straight line: "It circles and twists and turns corners and goes off on long curves. It boomerangs back on itself. It's a knave and rogue. It's all the things I'm blamed for being" (227).

The gambler will achieve immortality only when his circular images, like God's, move into the universal. Only in the spiritual perfection of heavenly existence does the circle stop whirling, the cards drop on the floor, the pattern become fixed forever; and this is possible for him because, outside the gates, he declared his intention to join the cards, the fragments of his will, in unity and to "join the unity to the will of the man who made me a gambler." Heaven then becomes the place of the intuitive knowledge sought in cards; the place where "You'll understand why men dance at death, and the symbolism of twelve men and their master. For in heaven one learns a lot. The hell of hell is that the soul endures so much and finds out nothing" (241).

Just as the stone circle proved a welcome place of meditation for a very Christian God, so the pagan symbol *twelve* now merges with the twelve disciples of Christ. A third prevalent number in *Cards of the Gambler* is the number three, another of those which unites the old and the new. The linear triad from earliest knowledge has meant primarily some kind of unity as in the all-embracing beginning, middle, end; past, present, future; earth, sky, atmosphere; terrestrial, celestial, infernal; and, as in the Hegelian dialectic, yes, no, reconciliation. For *Cards of the Gambler* the triangular religious ternary of destruction, creation, and preservation has special significance. The Oriental faces of the twelve dancers and the similarity of wheel and circle evoke associations with Eastern religions. The Buddhist triad of tree (life), tomb (death), and wheel (self-creation, self-preservation, and harmony) and the Indian triad of Brahma (Creator), Shiva (Destroyer), and Vishnu (Preserver) have similarities which lurk near the gambler's conscience when, surprised at meeting God in a pub, he responds with "You may be the avatar, the mask for the Unknown," for the Vishnu was said to come to earth in saintly guise. The gambler quickly blames fear of the Unknown on a guilty heart, on the suspicion that each person has a part in crime. God reminds the gambler of the story of a "man and a woman, a serpent and a tree"; but the gambler persists that such explanation provides no answers: "Who was the serpent? What fruit grew on the tree when you walked in the garden? And where in each one of us does the memory of the garden end and the memory of the sin begin?" (31).

God responds with a quotation from the Book of Job, uttered by the vanquished and despairing Job upon the ash heap: "I know that thou canst do all things, and no thought is hid from thee. . . . With the hearing of the ear I have heard thee but now my eye seeth thee. Therefore I reprehend myself, and do penance in dust and ashes" (31, 32). The gambler has until now failed to realize that sin and retribution, as in the story of Adam and Eve who heard God's voice, does not complete the Bible; that Job's guiltless suffering taught him, who saw God, that all was not revealed in the garden; that man cannot know all the divine purposes; that to expect God's purposes to be limited to individual sin is in itself sacrilege. God's immediate purpose in the gambler's life is to baptize his child, an action which He determines upon even though the gambler, unlike Job, should refuse to admit defeat.

While the twelve men dance their ring-o'-rosy song, God as the thirteenth man sits immobile. His beautiful voice saying "Some of them don't even know I'm buying the drinks. Some do know and don't care," and his clerical attire identifies him as God before He admits it. He exemplifies the Unmoved Mover when he adds, "But I can afford it and it gives me great pleasure to set things moving" (27). The God stereotype becomes amusing when the contact man (Death) explains God's sudden disappearance ("He's a fast mover"), his retreat to the mountain of the cromlech ("He likes altitude"), and his suggestion to have lunch there ("His reverence has certain winged waiters always at his disposal"); and one time God comments, "I suppose I have some experience in arbitration." In the restaurant the thirteenth man— God—reads French beautifully while the gambler squirms under the eyes of the six ex-partners who own his coat and car. Their baleful, conspirational glance drives the doctor to make his first wish, success at cards.

Of the third wish, the thirteenth man responds, "I've heard something like that before"; for he knows well the thoughts of the gambler: "It would be the joke of generations of wry peasants who had imagined the devil thwarted and imprisoned in the crooked branches of an apple-tree." And, though God grants the wish, He brands it "lunatic" (68).

The three wishes exemplify the religious triad: to destroy his opponents at cards (Destruction), "to bring life into dark, weeping rooms" (Creation), and to maintain a secret unlimited power through his one important possession, his car (Preservation). Having therefore established a local triad of man (gambler) in a garden of eternal life (his healing power) with power over evil (death, when it sits in his car), the thirteenth man vanishes from the face of the earth and does not again appear to the gambler, though Death appears often and in many guises.

The gambler's attempt to thwart death by imprisoning him in the apple-tree-car establishes Death and the Devil as one, and later, when the gambler dies and goes to purgatory, the dominant spirit of purgatory is the same Death he has learned to know well. The character of Death is a delightful conglomeration of the traditional, the fantastic, and the peculiarly Kiely creature. He enters through a disorderly bar, a diminutive Palace of Pandemonium, where the master barman has succumbed to intoxication; when Death pushes the bell three times, in contrast with God's summons, nothing happens. His informant, he claims, is a dark horse; and, though he has secret information, he modestly disclaims greatness; for he is not a prime mover: "I don't set anything moving. I come in at the end and buy up anything that's left."

At first appearance, Death is "a stout, red-faced man, middle age, middle height, wrapped in good brown tweeds that made his body look stouter and his face more rosy, wearing a loud check cap with the peak at a merry angle above his dark dancing eyes, carrying a huge brief-case" (35). He could be a bookie, a commercial traveler, or a man making contacts in the hotels, but the gambler learns later that, when Death appears, he has borrowed a recent corpse. He maintains a kind of duality of mind with his own interests to serve while he temporarily adopts the attitudes of the deceased but in his own right he has a keen sense of humor, and appreciation of the bizarre, and—the infallible Kiely touch—a lofty knowledge of books and ready quotations. His briefcase contains books, bones, and newspaper clippings describing his work; a favorite book from which he reads aloud is Dostoevsky's *Crime and Punishment;* another is Keats's poetry; and certainly he thrives on such grinding poverty and brutality as that of Marmeladov in Dostoevsky's novel and on the pale consumption of the youthful poet. He regrets that, in spite of Keats, no one wants to be eased by him; he dislikes both suicides and efforts to escape him. When the gambler names heroes and martyrs as those who face death calmly, he jeers, "Did you ever see a calm hero or a cool martyr?" But Death is realistic; while the gambler's fear of death, because he has broken his bargain, becomes submerged in sorrow over the death of his son, the contact man informs him "Mercy isn't my business." The gambler's life after the pact is one long dance, and death is his partner.

II   *The Dance of Death Undone*

The old folk tale appropriately cast the character of the doctor as professional contender with death, while the gambler with each turn of a card casts toward creation or destruction of his fortune. Then, having been granted occult powers, the doctor symbolizes the old dichotomy of fate (in cards) versus free will (in cures). The cards which he calls the fragments of his will, themselves in three colors and many patterns, represent a variety of desires and occupations. In medieval Christian art, black stands for penitence; red, for love; white, for purity. The path of spiritual ascension can be symbolized by the addition of a fourth color: penitence (black), illumination and revelation (white), suffering and love (red), and glory (gold). The emblems of the four suits in cards represent four types of earthly pursuits: diamonds, for material or spiritual wealth; clubs, as maces or scepters for power as in government; spades, or swords, for justice through military strength; hearts or goblets, for the priesthood.[6]

At the beginning of the story the gambler, having been negligent of all God's gifts, is a very desolate Adam with dominion over nothing. He has made desultory efforts to hire someone else to tend his garden, but his alone in suburbia is choked with weeds; he does not lead a "regular" life, he does not love his wife nor provide for his children. The wife's cousin, when he returns from having lost everything, ironically greets him with "Where in God's name have you been?"; but he calls his reflection in the mirror a phantasm and cannot take himself in his husband-father role seriously. Having willed his fall, he has now achieved supreme contentment through total destruction; counting himself among the damned, he need no longer strive against damnation. To seal his fate, he kisses the wife's cousin, whom he loves, and thereby destroys, he claims, the one beautiful and pure memory of his life—a childhood scene of shared innocence and laughter.

If gambling has the value he attributes it—to prove that he is not afraid of the dark—the proof is not final until the last attachments to the light are dissolved. Having met God, his question, "Why me?" remains to be answered indirectly by Death, who reads, apparently from Yeats, "I see always this one thing, that in practical life the mask is more than the face." [7] Those masks of respectability, in all suburbia, have irritated the gambler to rebellion. The devil points the irony of the gambler's counting his lost practice, reputation, and friends as less important than a trivial moment's kiss; but for the gambler the difference lies between sincerity and pretense. He resents the pretense of social respectability which others maintain through exactly those avenues of work, reputation, and friends.

With his first request assuring him victory, the gambler seeks his former companions, who vote, since he failed to pay his debts of coat and car, whether to admit him to their group. The history professor, later reviewing the evening's events, speaks closely to the gambler's heart: "You see, the trouble with this country is that we pride ourselves overmuch on a certain sort of morality, sixth and ninth commandments, you know what I mean; and we have absolutely no notion of common honesty in business dealings, no commercial morality whatsoever. In that respect our neighbours, the British, are our moral superiors" (80).

Having through the intervention of God been reborn into respectability, the doctor for seven years keeps his bargain with Death, always recognizing him whether he sits at the foot or at the head of the bed. But he soon realizes that he has gained nothing in understanding the *why* of human existence, particularly the meaning of the beloved dark woman's life and death. "Would he know everything on the day he broke his bargain with Death?" he wonders; and, having admired the courage of a young Spanish woman in dire need of a resurrected husband, he debates the problem with Death, now sitting at the head of the bed. He asks whether he can cure by an effort of will in spite of Death, and Death replies, "You're looking for dangerous knowledge." He moves the bed, endangering himself to help the woman, and disregards Death's quiet protest, "She'll be on my hands soon enough." He sacrifices the girl to Death, now wearing the body of a lecherous old man; and he learns only after his own death that the recovered husband, a few minutes after the doctor's hasty departure, had discovered the woman dead in another man's bed. He had not observed that, when Death touches a person, the person dies; such failures prove the futility of the third request.

Having broken the bargain, the doctor yearns backward to the time when he gambled without money, when the dark woman was alive, when he had known "the joy of a simple monetary ruin with no lunatic mysteries, no bones broken or lives lost in bad bargains." Passive people waiting for a bus, now that he is aware of death's danger to himself, resemble figures cut in wood because he is physically alive more than they. The bus journey leaves him detached, observant; he sees life continue around him in repeated activities of other people. Seeing Death sitting beside him, he leaps from the bus, waits for the *téléferique* in a restaurant where the food he eats seems alive: "The wine was white and sour, the meagre blood of small white grapes. He ate sandwiches made from coarse brown bread and raw fat bacon" (144). He experiences fear of plunging to death from the high *téléferique* to jagged rocks below; and, from this preview of heaven, he turns into a ranting maniac until the pinnacle of fear is passed. Like a discharged murderer gloating over evil done with impunity, he takes a hotel room with new joy, only to wake to find Death, in the guise of a local hero, sitting at the foot of his bed.

At Lourdes, he describes for Death the childhood experience with sin, going to confession every second Friday to say "Father, I disobeyed my parents once, and I was late for school twice, and I copied my sums from another boy's exercise, and I broke my wee brother's toy horse, and that's all, father" (152). Reacting to the gambler's claim that he wants to rediscover this innocence once before he dies, Death in his role of Death and devil humorously replies, "The word embarrasses me," but the doctor insists he wants "to return to innocence, to the moment of pure faith." This time, joining the pilgrims at the shrine, he walks away from Death. The news of his son's death, brought by a kindly Jesuit friend of the boy, shatters the peace of the grotto and precipitates a hasty return to Ireland. It marks also his determination to use his powers to ease death in the slums, and he learns that the unfinished work and the problems not solved, not fear of death, urge men to avoid death.

The greatest affront to human dignity from unsightly odors and smells and fetid, wretched poverty and ignorance can be found in a grimy restaurant where the doctor surreptitiously passes his plate to a starving tatterdemalion. He returns to this earthly hell to recapture through association with his former disgrace the treasured memory of the dark woman who represents on the adult scene not the original innocence but a second plateau of innocence before his pact with God. The gesture of proffered food, accepted with a glance of moral superiority, promotes the doctor to another level of understanding; he realizes "the folly of his search for a place where men had loosened the knots that tied them to life, where men could fool Death by forestalling him with ironic resignation" (173).

This same searching the past for happiness supplies the identities he conjectures of persons who could be the big man who cuts the deck for a nine of cards each time the doctor cuts a seven. The stranger takes the gambler-doctor to his fortified and secluded home, where the bartered soul has gone into hiding intentionally to attract attention; ironically, the children are most susceptible to the magnetic attraction of the barricaded and peculiar. This attraction of children too deceptively could be construed as "Suffer the little children to come unto me" until the gambler and big man engage in a circular card game in which the strange man's visage changes with each denomination. As the king of diamond's, his face is "all acute angles, diamond-shaped eyes smouldering with hostile greed"; next he is a "monstrous black king, thick, brutal lips, eyes that in green jungles had gloated over the flogging of screaming slaves"; for the cards graphically project human desires. A subsequent encounter with Death brings the explanation of the big man's collapse at the gambler's erroneous naming of God; a modern Faust, he had been killed by the fury of the dark horse, but his supernatural powers have revived the legendary God-Devil contention.

Admittedly dead to any normal life, the gambler desires of Death an extension to expire first in all memories and sentiments; but Death dubs such desire pure vanity and foolishness: "Somewhere you'll be remembered," he insists. But, when the doctor then determines to return unannounced to the childhood scene, he wears a slight accidental cut on his right hand; death has entered his body.

At the airport, a fitting location for departure for heaven, while seeking to exact the power of the third wish by locking Death in his car, the gambler walks off through the fields and discovers seven cyclists attempting a steep-hill competition. He watches three deaths without realizing the futility of the third request until he reads in a late newspaper about the discovery of his car which contained the body of a well-known recluse.

His whereabouts unknown to others, he returns to a small North Ireland town to stay with an ancient woman of more than ninety who had been his nurse. Having sent money every month, he has been an unknown benefactor to her; and she allows him without question—because she no longer questions anything—to complete here the circle of his days just as his father many years before had watched the small child return from his walk by a different route from that of departure and boast, "I've made a circle on the surface of the world." Like T. S. Eliot in *Little Gidding,* he has recognized that

> We shall not cease from exploration
> And the end of all our exploring
> Will be to arrive where we started
> And know the place for the first time.[8]

On the fifteenth night he is so refreshed and strengthened by renewal of old associations that he realizes he can go now to that particular green place by the sea to confront once more the most sacred memory. The prayer he teaches the crying child,

> I am the son of God
> He who says these words in memory of me
> Shall never take the fever or the ague (212)

embraces another mystic three—that of body, mind, and soul. This triad implies that the end of dying is the threshold of potential rebirth. The number fifteen, however, has long been associated with the devil; as the gambler thinks about the prayer, Death overtakes him on a stairway—in antiquity, a symbol of the way of heavenly ascent.

III *The Threshold of Beyond*

The Prologue of *Cards of the Gambler* effects a view from the sky above, like the perspective of one in heaven, gradually sweeping concentrically to focus on the West Donegal cottage of the ninety-year-old Gaelic storyteller. To this same celestial prospect the gambler has arrived at the end of the novel; the novel, then, achieves the circular motion conveyed by its dominant symbol.

A novelist seeking to describe the journey of man's soul from earth to purgatory to heaven often draws his concepts from a variety of mythological, biblical, Dantean, Miltonic, or other sources, and he can conveniently make his picture of other worlds, even more advantageously than those of this one, the vehicle for his message. Should Dantean or other similarities appear, the reader must be alert to avoid supplanting the intended theme with a facile traditional one. *The Cards of the Gambler* is not, strictly, a novel with a Faustian theme; nor is it a novel of sin and retribution, though both could be deduced by the undiscerning critic. The gambler does not sell his soul to the devil; he is as much in the hands of God as of Death. Nor do God and Death tally his sins to mete out eternal punishment for temporal errors.

Assuredly the gambler has committed sins of omission as far as earthly treasures should concern him. In regard to retribution and the three wishes and why he merits heaven, it can be observed that he has paid for his "crimes" while enjoying the dubious patronage of God and Death. If the gambler is to derive pleasure from gambling, he has in that wish frustrated his own efforts; assured success soon deprives him of competitors. The wish for success in healing the sick achieves ultimately, in spite of Death's intervention, more good for others than for the doctor; and his pleasure in success is offset by the devil's actively causing accidents which kill the persons the doctor most cherishes—the woman he loves and his son—though in purgatory he must ask himself whether he willed the woman's death in order to preserve her memory inviolate. The third wish is as futile as containing evil in an apple tree. The three wishes merely redemonstrate that man will never have all the answers, that no power can make of this earth a heaven, and that peace comes only after death.

The gambler at the beginning of the novel has not sought either God or devil; they exist in his life in spite of initial indifference on his part, as if man is always destined to play third party to the God-devil binary. But the doctor's is the forced indifference of the intellectually rebellious; he is too morally conscious of his self-willed damnation, as he terms it, and too morally unselfish in exercising his restorative powers to have achieved with Death the Dr. Faustus-Mephistopheles rewards of earthly pleasures. Having never cared for middle-class respectability, he permits the delights of wealth and fame to accrue to his wife, who, prior to the doctor-gambler's pact with Death, remained complacent because of satisfaction with dependence on her mother and allowed an actual usurpation by the mother-in-law of the father's role as provider. (The wife is quick to remind her husband, when money is plentiful, that her mother's will helped too.)

The gift of the two wishes is required eventually to shake him out of his lethargy; not until earthly pleasures are both rejected (before the pact) and exhausted (as much as he wishes, after the pact) will he understand that he understands nothing, will he challenge death and become *l'homme engagé*. His wife, more an automaton than a person, exemplifies all the mores of suburbia which he most hates; she has not time to express sorrow at his death but devotes her energies to suppressing the story of his death, not because there is anything wrong with it, but because he did not die at home sensibly in bed and because the death could be construed, therefore, as a little strange.

The purgatory to which he goes is Miltonic with two pillars and "pathetically medieval" horrors beyond. His sin, he is told, occurred in a moment when he would have condemned other souls to homelessness. He suspects hell is being alone; his punishment is to remember and desire the past, but the uncontrolled memories of beautiful scenes turn ghastly or stop before completion. The voice of Death who knows him well assures him that his hell "would be shaped like a respectable suburb." The gambler can elaborate on this analogy: "wealthy, ignorant, pious people . . . careful about the sort of books they read. . . . They'd all hate each other . . . over a killing these nice people would in secret lick their lips, lovingly syllabling the names of the poisons, the nature of the knife, the details of the punishment of the scapegoat killer. . . . In that respected neighbourhood those irreproachable people would live in faultless houses and sit in circles congratulating one another" (230). The wife who ostentatiously commits no wrong is the very epitome of the middle-class morality he hates. These people of suburbia have no will of their own, no cards to represent the fragments of their will, no souls to be dramatically saved; their platitudinous lives never vibrate with dynamic tricolor patterns. Sin is pharisaic; it is guile clothed in respectability.

A white road going north ends speculation on this type of

living hell. At the airport, the involvement in good and evil in each one of man is symbolized by the two faces—one black, one white—indicative of the two souls of good and evil in even the dullest man. Heaven is mostly white light with the traditional Peter as the clerk who retells, with many humorous interjections from giant and doctor, the story of Saint Christopher.[9] Now a twelve-foot pilot, the man of many silver plaques in numerous automobiles, who carried the sins of the world across the river, evokes associations once more with a pre-Christian ritual, the symbolic washing away of the community's ills in pagan tribes.

Heaven, the gambler learns, is the place of final knowledge where the third power, or resolution of dualism, can be found, a place to "find out the exact differences between ending and beginning, sin and sacrifice, darkness and light."

Like the pagan statues in the old Georgian country house converted to Jesuit training, as described in *Land Without Stars* and *There Was an Ancient House*, the identity of Saint Christopher, as well as the symbols of pagan and Christian mythology, unite the past and present and develop the theme of the continuity of man's desire, especially the desire to know. Sir James Frazer, lyrically concluding *The Golden Bough*, wrote that magic, religion, and science are nothing but supersessive theories of thought.[10] They are man's attempts to know what lies beyond the threshold of beyond. *The Cards of the Gambler* is a story of man's search for a final answer.

CHAPTER 9

Where Few Shall Enter:
There Was an Ancient House

F OR those who construed Kiely's withdrawal from seminary and his subsequent aspersion of fictional religious hypocrisy as rejection and denial of his clerical past, *There Was an Ancient House,* as well as sympathetic characterization of clergy in other novels and short stories, should convince them of the error of their critical ways. The novel is a study of one year of religious discipline and the varied personalities of those who submit to it; of the eighteen who begin novitiates, only thirteen at the end of the year have persevered.

I *The Narrow Way*

"It was a white world," the first sentence of *There Was an Ancient House,*[1] marks the transference of young Jim MacKenna to a strange, colorless world where both actions and thoughts are regimented toward achievement of the clear radiance of spirituality. To establish the polarity between the external and the cloistered world, Kiely adopts, particularly at the beginning, a strained, rigidly controlled style, a Latinized vocabulary, and heavy quotations from and allusions to saints and authors of religious treatises. Not until the second half of the book, when the point of view shifts temporarily to the girl friend of another neophyte, Brother Barragry, does the style become relaxed, familiar, and companionable. For the novices, the grave aspiration toward the ideal of holiness weighs upon them and makes them extremely conscious of their own unworthiness; their strain relaxes only slightly with greater familiarity with the routine until the holiday near the end of the first year; by this time, the novices have recognized the possibilities for individuality in a strict religious order; and Kiely's style grows easier accordingly.

Stylistic constraint best evidences itself in the examples of humor. The father Magnov, or Master of Novices, speaking to probationers, instructs while he welcomes: "Father Willy Doyle, the Jesuit who died almost a martyr's death when he was a chaplain in the first world war, was fond of saying that if people in the world only knew the happiness of the religious life they'd break down the doors to get in. That was why I kept the front door so carefully open when all you healthy young men were arriving" (20)—and such a statement brings eighteen uneasy smiles. Informal conversation becomes a matter of condescension: "brace you up" and "pep-talk" from the Magnov are described as "slang words, gently, neatly nipped off, crisp celery snapping, by lips more accustomed to the words of God, to the breviary's sonorous Latin, the words of the Mass. . . (22). When the Magnov informs them that they will hear interesting talk, "at the times when talk is the principle," the novices strive gallantly to appear other than frightened of themselves and of everything around them; and they respond with "a nervous eighteen-barrelled laugh." Not until the second half of the book does Kiely verbalize the phenomenon of these reactions: "In a strained silent world anything was funny."

The geographic isolation of the old Georgian country house of an ancient Anglo-Irish lord,[2] closed off from the surrounding countryside by bogland and clochar, or oak grove, and the sensitivity about the remote history of former life in the house contribute to the atmosphere of constraint and seclusion. The setting at Emo Paric, the ancestral mansion of a lord of former times described in *Land Without Stars*, is approximately fifty miles southwest of Dublin. Serviced by lay brothers who do much of the domestic and related work of the religious community, the seminary is self-sufficient; newspapers are forbidden; and excursions to the outside world, such as hospital and poorhouse, are conducted for serious purposes of service, instruction, and recreation.

A Latinized vocabulary also emphasizes monastic seclusion. Books come from the "ad usum"; externs are people outside the cloister; "semper," the first word of "semper deo gratias," or "always thank God," gently admonishes a slight departure from, or adjures adherence to, regulation; the "ambulacrum" is a long hallway; the "menology" or biographies of saints is read aloud at dinner; the "cameratas" are second-floor living quarters; the specific term "discipline" as opposed to general routine means self-inflicted scourge on the right shoulder or the wearing of a barbed chain on the right forearm; "exercitants" are engaged in a particular activity such as retreat; "to spem" is to hope for or to forecast; "animae" are neophytes and "angeli" are older students assigned to guard neophytes; and "villa" means holiday, the Irish term for vacation. Additional familiarity with Latin requires thinking in the language of the mass; and the thoughts of Mac-Kenna and Barragry, from whose viewpoints the major portions of the novel are presented, are larded with Latin phrases for routine activities. Translated carefully, the Latin serves purposes of humor as well as erudition.

Kiely's predilection for quotations, much apparent in earlier novels, acquires in *There Was an Ancient House* its natural environment, where MacKenna is a poet and Barragry a former journalist. Now the quotations and the study of religious lives provide a frame of reference for spiritual guidance and for personal problems. G. K. Chesterton wrote of the pope as a builder of bridges, of the closed mind as a padded-cell mentality; Thomas à Kempis, refusing to let semantics substitute for holiness, stressed the feeling, rather than the definition, of charity and the grace of God. Joris Karl Huysmans declared he must begin living in the clerical world "by throwing prejudice overboard." Bret Harte provides nuances of pronunciation for voice production. Quotations from an Essene prior, John Milton, Robert Browning, Cardinal Newman, Patrick Pearse, James Stephens, and numerous other poets and scholars fill the conversation of the novices, especially MacKenna's, whose response "Wise as the serpent, simple as the dove" to characterize the saints elicits from Barragry a dry "With your usual aptness, Brother MacKenna."

Part III of the novel, entitled "Manresa" with reference to the cave of retreat of the founding Father Ignatius Loyola, details a multitude of examples from the lives of the saints and other spiritual leaders. In Ulster, Patrick minded sheep; and Kevin of Glendalough, to preserve his chastity, tumbled the pursuing Kathleen down a cliff into water. Simeon Stylites lived on a pillar; Margaret of Cortona disfigured her criminal body; and the recital of deeds and thoughts of religious leaders helps novices adjust to the demands of their vows.

Because of the aptness of Edmund Spenser's *Faerie Queene,* Spenser provides the epigraph and title and occurs most frequently of nonreligious [3] authors in the thoughts of MacKenna and Barragry. When MacKenna recites, "There was an auncient house not far away,/ Renowned throughout the world for sacred lore,/ And pure unspotted life . . . ," Barragry remembers the house of holinesse where an aged "syre hight Humilta" opened the door and Zele was a "francklin faire and free." In the midst of menial kitchen chores, Barragry's recitation of Spenser eases the slop-laden way to feeding the seminary pigs: "So few there bee, that chose the narrow path, or seeke the right: all keepe the broad high way, and take delight with many rather for to go astray, and be partakers of their evil plight, than with a few to walk the rightest way." [4]

There Was an Ancient House stands in direct contrast to *Honey Seems Bitter;* as a study of a year's novitiate, plot in *There Was an Ancient House* is subordinate to character; suspense is the question how long one can tolerate the discipline of the order. Brother MacKenna has been shielded from the world since his first communion; Brother Barragry, MacKenna's best friend, is older, a barrister, an experienced journalist who has entered the novitiate independent of family encouragement and prompted by feelings of guilt. The novel then chronicles the trials of individuals of contrasting personalities being molded into men of God: Barragry, the gently cynical man of the world; MacKenna, inexperienced, innocent, devout. Regarding the question of perseverence, some, like Petit, Begley, and Foley, can wear piety like a soutane; they easily conform to the requirements of the order. Of the others who doubt, the worldly and mature Barragry is the only one who has the freedom to admit his doubt in conversation.

One weekend Barragry's girl almost comes to him. Her failure within sight of the ancient house subtly demonstrates that Barragry must reach his own decision, if it is to be the right one, about returning to the world. Physical illness determines for MacKenna his final departure from the order, but he leaves with regret and enters the new world of the hospital with his metaphors not now so much drawn from books as from the actions and conversation of his former religious brethren. [5]

Who shall choose the narrow way marked by Spenser or who shall cross the bridge which Chesterton metaphorically saw built by the Pontifex is the question which ruffles the calm of Mac-Kenna's, and others', meditation. MacKenna at his first communion prayed to be a priest and saw the monstrance like a burning bush; on his first neophytical morning, he wakens to the sight of his white-curtained cubicle and remembers "He had always wanted to be separate and different, to feel as he now felt: white, curtained-off, sacrosanct, protected" (9); but he suffers a feeling of unworthiness. An adolescent experience with a forward girl haunts him as evidence of his impurity, and the only consolation directly applicable to his experience comes, not from any life of a saint, but from his friend Frankie's grandmother, who insisted "the boy who had a true vocation could never lose his purity all the way."

Barragry, the monk with a past and the late vocation, entered after a sexual sin which continues to haunt him because confession ensures forgiveness and because he is not sure his vocation is not a self-imposed punishment. Memories of the world intrude on his spiritual exercises; he finds himself too easily thinking "When I get back to the world. . . ." Taking his problem to the Magnov, he hears a gentle warning against remorse about remorse, the sin of which he is already aware. When striving toward godliness seems utterly futile, Barragry tempers frustration for others with the soothing admonition: "Let us not aspire to be more than Christians"; but he cannot derive comfort from his own counsel.

No matter of class distinction, the origins of those who elect the religious life vary extremely. Brother O'Rhattigan made his decision as a young coffin-maker required to open a once-buried coffin containing poisoned liquefied flesh; Brother Barnes talks of visits from the queen and of goose for Michaelmas dinner, whereupon Brother Nangle responds that his people had not kept geese. Brother O'Brien claims he came to write a novel, having never found one in the world to please him; Brother Lacy in the world had been a school's champion tennis player; Brother Matthews keeps the soul of a poorhouse inmate alive with stories of race horses. Brothers singly and together can inquire in the vernacular, "Why in the name of Jasus am I here," but all are certain that the way to God is through silence, humility, solitude, prayer, mortification, and renunciation.[6]

II *Ours Shall and Ours Shall Not*

The strict rules for novices govern not only actions but also thoughts. There is little privacy; both outgoing and incoming letters are read by the Magnov, a custom frankly dubbed espionage by the recalcitrant Brother Frawley. The Jesuit spiritual existence can be summed up in the requirements of "community life, silence, strict rules, no holidays at home, poverty, chastity, obedience." In contrast with other orders which permit holidays at home, these rules seem unnecessarily stringent; but they assure in community life, Brother MacKenna reflects, a guarantee against the solitary existence of the country priest who often has no one of comparable education with whom he can communicate.[7] The Jesuits impose silence at particular times, but the Cistercians make it almost constant. Jesuit policy includes the "ne tangas"[8] rule, but Brother Frawley, who chafes sorely under the discipline, wonders how one can play football and yet observe a rule about no body touching another body.

The quarters of charity sessions with the Magnov require that each brother report the faults he has observed in other brothers; failure to report a fault—and Brother MacKenna can find no fault in Brother Barragry—is in itself a fault in not helping a brother know himself. The Magnov smiles: "Brother Barragry has been made perfect in a short time." In his responses, the Magnov agrees and disagrees, helps the accuser to tolerance and the accused toward perfection:

"Father, I think Brother MacKenna makes too much noise in the camerata."

"A serious thing, brother. True silence is more than a mere matter of not speaking. Still, we're men, not mice, nor ghosts." (69)

Another routine, the "examen" of conscience, perhaps tries the faith most severely, necessitating as it does critical scrutiny of one's attitude toward self, others, and God. No random thinking is permitted; subjects for meditation are carefully prepared before the session to help the novice toward spiritual perfection. Constant examination of the self and regulation of every movement, including custody of the eyes to indicate repose of the soul, inevitably brings a flood of depression known as the novitiate blues, for which everyone concerned urges prayers for perseverance. Even Donnelly, a second-year student and organist, suffers severe depression during the long, sodden retreat. Perseverance provides humor when Donnelly observes that the lay Brother Hazlitt,[9] who is bent double with age, supports "himself simultaneously leaning on a stick and tugging his coat-tail." In sixty or seventy years with the Order, "he was pretty sure of perseverance." For Donnelly, who cannot compose even a cribbed sermon, perseverance means continuing in spite of the agonies of public speech. His sermon, if nothing else does, proves him a true religious:

"In all our sufferings," Donnelly said, "we should remember what our Divine Lord suffered on the cross for our sins. Not only will that memory help us the better to bear our own trials but we will gain great grace by realising how much our Lord suffered for us, and by joining our sufferings to his sufferings and the sufferings of the holy martyrs who also suffered and died. We should say," said Donnelly desperately, suffering himself, feeling like a martyr, "Thy holy will be done." To pad things out a bit he added: "On earth as it is in heaven." (81)

But perseverance waxes extremely difficult when even holy enthusiasm becomes suspect; should one repeat the same prayer five hundred times, the fear of vainglory must counter his pride in achievement. Inordinate affection for any activity or creature, even the birds which the ornithologist Brother Guinan loves, must be suspected as sinful. MacKenna, who fears he has an inordinate affection for poetry, argues with himself and Barragry about whether he should surrender his notebook of carefully preserved specimens of poetry written over the past several years. When the poetry may be amateurish or unworthy, citations of brother Jesuits such as Gerard Manley Hopkins offer little consolation. At last when MacKenna takes courage and conscience in hand to confess his fear to the Magnov, there follows one of the most skillfully touching scenes of the book. The Magnov graciously introduces other topics to still MacKenna's anxiety, blending humor and counsel in a casual manner so that ultimately the magnitude of MacKenna's secret occupation dims to harmlessness and then glows into happiness. For the first time the holy house is home.

Voice production every morning means walking the clochar's

twisted paths and practicing vowel sounds, for which practice
the painful test comes in reading aloud from the rostrum at dinner in the refectory, with corrections by Peesoc, or Pater Socius,
Father Companion of the Magnov. Brother MacKenna knows his
North of Ireland vowels never will conform to the uniformity of
pronunciation demanded by the order. Brother Barragry, whose
vowels are part of his perfect Oxford accent and his respected
lineage, unexpectedly fails his speech test elsewhere. In a visit
to a poorhouse, he winces under the remark of an inmate that he
has the true twang of a Dublin jackeen.

The weapons for mortification of the novices' flesh are casually
introduced by the angelus on a quiet country walk: "a small five-
tailed whip of hard white cord" for striking the shoulder blade;
"a chain of fine wire with points turned inward so that it resem-
bled a fragile elongated harrow" for wearing at required times
on the right forearm. The novices suffer an inclination to laugh
and then mild shame, but they soon accept the purposes of mortification to teach humility and to remind them of the suffering of
the Lord.

Submission of will and judgment in all things short of sin,
another requirement, means that one does not reprove a brother,
even to point out that the brother has temporarily failed to submit
will and judgment. To be esteemed a fool for Christ's sake, if
this is the way subjection appears to the outside world, also prepares the true religious for holy life. But to be esteemed a fool
for Christ's sake—the third degree of humility—can come through
a variety of ways, especially, as Barragry learns to his dismay
during the poorhouse visit, it can come through holy poverty.
A pauper begs money for a jar (a pint of stout) when he can slip
away from the supervising nuns to the nearest pub. Barragry
protests he has no money, but his mind rushes ahead to the
priesthood of the future when he would be approached by numerous "touchers" on city streets; and, refusing, he would see himself
judged by laymen, who would undoubtedly disparage the priests
who have "no time for the poor." Submission of will means that
the accused priest cannot defend himself.

Through all humiliations and difficulties, with pain, Latin, and
pronunciations, the doctrine of acceptance reminds the novices
of Christ's suffering: "Accept everything in return for the gift of
perseverance, for the grace of advancement in the spiritual life,

of living and dying in the holy habit, of the company for all eternity of Christ and His saints. Abandon everything . . . in order to gain everything" (98). So much total commitment, even with prayers for perseverance, exacts too great a toll for three of the eighteen novices. Brother Frawley, the first to abandon the cause, has arrived with his special required clothing, which he calls "flummery," a constant reminder of his mother's sacrifice in the midst of her poverty to outfit him for the highest honor an Irish son can achieve. He resents his particular duty of feeding roaches [10] in the aquarium as much as he resents the criticism from quarters of charity. After a few days, he sums up the discipline with "Ours shouldn't be individual human beings at all." Striking an analogy between his chore and his vocation, he dubs community life a "sort of suffocating frog-sprawn quivering with prying eyes," though theoretically the mortification derived from such discomfort should improve the soul. As Frawley leaves what the literary MacKenna recognizes as a valley of squinting windows,[11] MacKenna, the last of the novices to see Frawley, watches from a window as if ironically to lend credence to the analysis. The very depressing scene and Frawley's "death to the religious life" cause a doubling of prayers for perseverance.

The second to depart, Brother Curran, who suffers an attack of novitiate blues at Christmas time, regards the walls around him as a prison. The Magnov calmly explains to MacKenna the departure of Curran as "Overstrain, dear brother. Too serious. Affecting his health"; but MacKenna, who is also the last person to see Curran, begins to grow superstitious about the connection between those departures and his own vocation. Brother Keown perseveres until the long retreat when incessant rain and holy silence prove the strain to be too heavy. "I'm in jail," he protests. "I've nausea from boredom. . . . [It's] no way for a man to live" (136).

Of those who remain, and who, apparently, always will persevere, Petit is a priestly stereotype. Described as "serious, intense, narrow-minded, the formidable Latin scholar, the solid man of prayer," he chooses a ponderous Latin text to read for voice production and fails utterly to understand Barragry's gentle banter. Brothers Foley and Begley almost duplicate Petit's attitudes and efforts. Also, Brother Nangle has a striking sense of humor; Guinan, a love of birds; Lagan, of boats; and Donnelly, of music. O'Rhattigan, the carpenter with a simple love of trees, keeps a picture of his girl in a swimsuit, and he represents "an extremity in the novitiate: a rugged rural character with a good deal of impulsive superstitious sanctity in him"—the superstition which would make of opening a mock-elm coffin an omen to warn that, since bodies dissolve into horrors, the soul must be saved. Barragry had earlier concerned himself with the anonymity of people in a small world where uniformity of rule and custom prevailed; but at the end of the long retreat, all recognize individuality which no rule or gown could disguise.

III   *Let Nothing Afright Thee*

The three truths which provide sermons and reflection for the long retreat—the first "I come from God"; the second, "I belong to God"; and the third, "I am destined for God"—contain the essence of serenity and repose. When Easter sunlight breaks the monotony of gloomy rainy days as depressing as Good Friday, the tension of the long retreat snaps; there are new joys in the meetings with missionaries and a famous Jesuit. For the first time, all novices agree "if the world only knew the happiness of religious life there wouldn't be a door in one sound piece in any ancient holy house in—but not of—the world." The villa, following the retreat, permits group excursions and visits from friends and relatives; MacKenna has become so well adjusted to the regimen that, when Frankie comes to visit, MacKenna seeks the protection of Barragry to preserve the order's dignity. But MacKenna suffers a secret pain; Barragry, remorse about remorse.

Just as MacKenna had fretted in silence over poetry, he suffers with any bending or sudden movement a stabbing "knitting needle in the spine." Under O'Brien's penetrating glance and probing questions, MacKenna realizes, as the pain becomes more frequent, that its effects have become observable. Finally, obeying the rule for reporting physical illnesses but doing so with a half-cynical reflection that the Jesuit body as well as the soul must be perfect, MacKenna goes to Dublin for X-rays. Returned and awaiting results, he finds unexpected kindness from the Father Rector who hands him, contrary to rules, a volume of Longfellow's poems, which he regards with reverence: "The book was a plush exotic worldling, alien on his table. For a whole day he looked at it lying there before he opened it. He had an uneasy feeling that he was doing something irrevocable" (227). As if proving that books, for MacKenna, evoke a religious response, the gesture marks his departure from the religious life.

With fear about what the future holds for him in pain and illness, MacKenna sentimentalizes the companionship of the Brothers and the attachments of the order, especially the peace and security there. As fear of departure replaces fear of perseverance, all things acquire new appearances and significances. The Magnov, gently revealing the serious results of the X-rays, seems suddenly frail. MacKenna "had always thought of him as tough, agile and wiry, but now he saw how the thin hand trembled, how the shoulder-blades bunched out under a worn glazed habit; and the skin around his Roman nose and high receding forehead was almost transparent. Asceticism and age? He felt he was walking with a saint" (228). The sorrow MacKenna feels then is the sorrow of breaking off these associations; it is not knowledge that separation from the religious life will be permanent.

Barragry, having sought counsel in the matter of withdrawing, had been advised to wait until after the long retreat. During the "villa" (vacation), he hesitates about a proper, casual way to break the news of his decision. When the group, during a sudden rain storm while on a bicycle trip, takes shelter in a pub, Barragry chafes under the estrangement of the gown which assures a separate room and the responsibility for having hushed the customers' conversations. He protests that the priests can win no people if partitioned from them; but no argument can dissuade the Magnov, who remains secure in his faith and in the rules of the order and who believes such action could be construed as betrayal of themselves, of the people, and of God. Returned to his "camerata" (dormitory), Barragry realizes the futility of examination of a conscience burdened with only one scruple; and late that night he walks out alone, taking absence without leave, to test the delights of the world before returning to it. Petit, fulfilling his duties, reports the excursion, though he could never know of Barragry's three free drinks graciously purchased by an already intoxicated citizen in the village pub. Petit's report removes the obstacle of telling the Magnov about his decision to leave. Again, there are no reprimands, but only understanding, assurances that much work remains to be done in the world, that though others must persevere and Barragry must go, the one year of religious life certainly fits God's plans for him.

In Dublin, MacKenna confesses to Barragry the haunting fear of his impurity, cites Frankie's grandmother's view of priests and purity, and adds, "I often think, perhaps it was because I wasn't good enough that this thing came on, this pain, disease." Barragry retorts that "She must have been a nasty old woman," and he judiciously refrains from additionally confusing MacKenna with an account of his own experiences.

Of the five who did not complete the two-year novitiate, three weakened because of the discipline; two, because they continued to apply their seminary standards of perfection to their experiences before they had entered. Barragry and MacKenna both could live in either cloister or world; in fact, Barragry calls his own ready adjustment a "hermaphroditic abnormality." But neither is able to accept the forgiveness of the church as absolution; both continue to feel, in spite of counsel, that a sin committed in the world must be atoned in the world. Barragry, therefore, cannot find peace until he returns to the girl; and MacKenna, who has never lost his love of the world's books, must in the world make some adjustment in his thinking about sexual sin. The new discipline of the hospital, as MacKenna relaxes custody of his eyes to observe the trim calves of a nurse, promises much. His closing thoughts, in the words of Saint Theresa, seem spoken, as he sinks into dream, by a young nurse "from a bud of a mouth, in a pert pear of face . . . 'Let nothing disturb thee, nothing affright thee, all things are passing; God only is changeless'" (244).

CHAPTER 10

Born and Damned:
The Captain with the Whiskers

KIELY'S seventh novel, *The Captain with the Whiskers*, is a study of the kind of evil—parental—which no law can punish and no love requite but for which fixation of guilt eludes the critical grasp. Is it evil because the captain mistreated his children, restrained and confined them in such demanding obedience that, in seeking freedom from restraint, they went wild? Or is evil, as in their actions after his death, a part of every person and the captain's kind of discipline the only mainstay against a world of evil? After everything has turned to pain and the absence of pleasure, after every horrible consequence of the captain's personality has had its unhappy parallel in a remembered phrase of the captain's conversations, Owen Rodgers, walking the scum-coated Liffey's South Wall far from the natural beauty of Magheracolton, reflects "Even now, I doubt if the captain was the monster." [1]

I *The Haunts of Evil*

The rural North Ireland coastal setting of the captain's domain witnesses the superior perspicacity with which he husbands the country's resources. He has built a huge sycamore- and hazel-shaded granite house with barns, byres, stables, carhouses, and haysheds behind it "like a fortified town" at exactly the enviable spot where the salmon-swollen Gortin River, having plunged from the mountains, slackens its pace and flows sedately into the sea. He has also swept into his grasp beyond the river another two miles of rich bottom land along with grazable foothills backing up under the mountains, and he includes in his tyrannical ownership the destinies of four cottiers and their families.

To appreciate the natural beauties of the valley, young Owen

Rodgers cycles from his home town, a fictional steep-hilled Omagh, along a curving road through the Gortin Gap where a sparkling spring with stone seat inscribed "Rest and be thankful" tempts wry speculation about the nature of the adjured thankfulness: for water, for rest, or for escape from the captain? Or is the allegorical journey of life assumed so miserable that a moment's rest climaxes all joyful expectancies? Approaching the captain's house renders Owen Rodgers awestruck: a seemingly motionless horse and rider vanish as if swallowed by the ground; the leaves on the Bingen trees are dry and brittle even in summer; the glittering seven-windowed span of the captain's forceful, squared house possesses him with the fascination of evil and contrasts with his home bungalow of mocking vivid orange in inexplicable curves. It is as if the captain's house shapes individuals into rigid patterns of angular discipline, while the Rodgers home allows laughter at life, freedom, relaxation, and the flow of music.

The description of the setting reveals a new level of maturity, ease, deftness, familiarity, and remarkable power to evoke horror in Kiely's style. The first person is intimate as well as convincing; the use of "you" is comfortably familiar. The general relaxation permits light humor and irony. Nearby Segully Mountain, for example, spawns a man whose unlicensed dog responds only to Irish and evades police detection by hiding on the mountain until the police are gone. Remembering the uneasy British police-Irish civilian strife, Owen Rodgers reflects, "A very Irish dog." Further, "You could damn near reach out of a window in Bingen and take a salmon by the gills" gives the flavor of vernacular exaggeration and makes the telling of the story a relation of local common knowledge. But speculation that "in some alchemic cellar [of the captain's house] a hunchbacked dwarf might follow the ways of evil" marks artistic conception beyond the range of mere narration. The creation of the very atmosphere of evil culminates in this novel a development first observed in *Honey Seems Bitter* and explains the fearful shudder which has drawn analogy with the style of Ambrose Bierce, though not only violent death but even more so violent or mutilated living concerns Kiely: Greta's "head burst in halves and a dock-labourer with the help of a young priest put it together again"; Edmund "emerged from his coma with a head that would never harden"; and the miller's soldier-son of *Dogs Enjoy the Morning* hovers near death with tropical fever raging in a body reduced to forty-seven pounds. The interior of the captain's house [2] dispels all hope for vital, human warmth. The mother never appears, and her whereabouts remains unknown; the only evidences of her presence are the folded, fan-shaped pieces of paper thrown into the unused fireplace. The cold, marble sitting-room mantel sports a stuffed snake and the picture of the captain in military uniform; and a gigantic "whatnot" displays tusks, horns, knives, and a shrunken skull. While the furniture of Bingen House invites reflection on death, the Rodgers home, again in contrast, enjoys a mother gently and laughingly present and contains a French horn whose need of a "night shift" invites association with warm, vibrant life. The effect of the Bingen House surroundings, where young Rodgers at his first approach has a feeling of being spied upon, drives him into guilty hiding to delay his arrival and imposes upon his young innocence the burden of sharing his friend's humiliation. The conversion of open, pleasant Owen Rodgers, the child of light and music, to lurking, secretive Peeping Tom Rodgers is the first thrust of the captain's evil into a life not his by genealogy. By association with the dungeonlike existence Owen has witnessed, the stones of the river on the return trip with water rushing over them sound like moving chains.

The awe of the inexplicable surrounds Bingen House also in the memory of the wizard Michael Doran, whose reputed necromancy fascinates Captain Conway Chesney and inspires him to emulation. The calculated deception which enabled Doran to cut off the finger of a rate collector and to keep the corpse of his sister unburied in his cabin in order to collect her pension, as told by the captain, becomes one with the antics of Gilles de Rais who committed more than two hundred corpses to the latrines of Paris. From the lips of the senior Rodgers, however, the preserved corpse loses its power and represents "advanced views on social welfare." Between these alternates and fortified with the knowledge that the wizard welcomed only his father as a visitor, Owen pursues the phantom to its origin and finds the locale, not even a mountain as it is called, but a bleak, deserted triangle of wet brown moorland with a house in ruins, open to wind and rain, a place from which Christians would flee not to avoid the devil but to avoid starvation. As the forlorn house of the magic man seems to banish the possibility of supernatural knowledge, however, Owen must ask himself what sort of fascination impels him to the evil captain's side, when he has no friend in Bingen House, and whether it is of the same variety as the captain's attraction to Gilles de Rais.

A series of known grotesqueries of his personal experience ranks with the captain's reduction of his own children to servitude and dejection before the eyes of Owen Rodgers. The guilt of unintentional association with perversion hovers over Owen who once, for example, danced with a girl who fainted from hunger on the ballroom floor and whose pointed breasts proved to be edible scooped-out heels of Vienna bread. The innocent children of happy homes may be sucked into the vortex of perversion as spectators rather than as participants while they try vainly to understand, like the necromancer communing with the dead, the intangibles of human motivation. Without committing evil, they become partakers of it through association; Owen asks, "Is black-avised, thoughtful detachment the worst perversion of all?"

Only a son for some unknown reason admitted to the captain's presence would question whether a motive other than friendship brought his father to Doran's doorstep; the senior Rodgers is the only person capable of viewing perversion with objectivity, of removing received humiliation to the sphere of the transgressor's limitations, of accepting rather than condemning man's pathetic attempts to achieve something that he thinks he desires. Although John Rodgers is a well-known, friendly man, the kind anyone could talk to and trust, he is, in knowing much and revealing little and in having access to restricted places, liable to create in some minds a suspicion that guarding the interests of many people requires duplicity. Owen's friend Kinnear's judgment of Owen as a "sinister, secretive bastard, like your father,"—though the father loves books, music, and people—is linked in this view with detachment and has more truth than jest.

The father, John Rodgers, remains at ease with the captain, when no one else does; in reality he despises the captain because "He was a reorganizer. That's a destroyer. He changed the old name of Magheracolton to Bingen" (141). As a gatherer of country ballads, John Rodgers cannot forgive this destruction of the beauty of the past. He adds, "There was a good song about the hills above Magheracolton."

In the meantime, the Rodgers household plays host to local

band rehearsals amid good drink and laughter with a mother whose only rebukes of their ribaldry urge them to greater charity. Listening to their jests and observing Dr. Grierson's visits when the father surreptitiously refills the priest's glass, Owen gives mute thanks for being the normal son of a normal man.

At the beginning of the novel, Owen's adolescent story of having been unjustly boxed on the ears for whispering in church brings from his father not a tirade against the aggressor but an expression of sympathy for him, the lonely ecclesiastical doctor who is too well educated to be either appreciated or understood and whose pleasures are in the past of another country. A short few years later, Owen understands some of those problems, largely through his father's sympathetic handling of Dr. Grierson's tendencies to drown his clerical loneliness in alcoholism. John Rodgers' objectivity permits him to accept without judgment, also, a clerical fondness for women for which alcohol, he claims, is an anesthetic. Part of Dr. Grierson's bitterness after an idyllic education at Louvain and Paris grows out of contention with his ecclesiastical superior, known as Higher Authority, who raises prize bulls and who has little else of spiritual or esthetic perception to recommend him.

Extremely sensitive, Dr. Grierson feels keenly the stupidity of his superior, who erroneously instructed him to prevent the marriage separation of a woman sexually frustrated and who refused to recognize a valuable art object because it was not garishly painted. On one side of Higher Authority's pulpit hangs Saint Dominic "with a face and figure like a dummy in a shop window" and on the other side Saint John the evangelist with a "hermaphroditical face and dressed in a red Dior creation." Owen had heard with much laughter a famous Dublin priest urge his congregation to gregariousness to guard its purity and to wear total-abstinence pins in reparation of others' intoxication; Dr. Grierson in one glance at the priest's book brands it "Piffle" and his character "A prig. A pain in the face."

The climax of Higher Authority's callousness comes on a day of cold, wet, discomfort and darkness with a sermon assuring his congregation that all of them will die; the person of Higher Authority confirms Dr. Grierson's understatement that death, even in the funereal black beer, is all around Ireland's people. Nor does kindness soften his criticism of his church. A hundred pounds

willed to the doctor by the captain does not alleviate the priest's
suspicion of the captain's collusion with the powers of darkness
and destruction; Dr. Grierson continues to consider him a devil
incarnate. With no illusions about humanity's inherent goodness
or the power of the priesthood to instill nonexistent goodness,
Dr. Grierson consoles himself as much as possible with his boat
and the companionship of the mellifluous John Rodgers.

From this demon-pervaded setting and among these diffusive
associations, the plot develops through the narration of Owen
Rodgers who, after the wicked captain dies of an unlikely accident, realizes he cannot become a doctor and instead manages
hotels and watches the effects of the captain's doleful influences.
The Chesney family falls into dissolution and Bingen House into
decay. The mother dies after a long illness with rambling mind;
the oldest son, Alfred, spends twelve months in jail for rape; the
second, Edmund, drives wildly into a bridge abutment and waits
out his remaining days whittling and sleeping in the sun; the third
son, Francis, becomes a bitter priest. Of the two daughters, the
beautiful and desirable Maeve becomes promiscuous; and quiet,
efficient Greta commits suicide.

Among Owen Rodgers' young friends, James Kinnear as legal
consultant continues to arbitrate suits brought against Alfred for
sexual offenses; and Jeff Macsorely yearns toward writing an
idyllic un-Irish novel, one which the Bingen House setting without the Bingen House people might have provided; he wants a
novel without mud and misery "in which every man and woman's
a virgin and nobody, not even a cow in a byre, has a baby" (282).
Owen, having fallen in and out of love with Lucy, Maeve, and
Greta in succession, having married Lucy who died, has moved
to Dublin where the industrial city provides manifold examples
of the destruction brought about by reorganization.

II *Evil Done with Impunity*

From *The Cards of the Gambler*,[3] two thoughts are carried
over into *The Captain with the Whiskers;* a limited morality
based on the sixth (adultery) and ninth (neighbor's husband)
commandments and a malicious personal triumph of having defied the deterministic forces of society and universe, the kind of
action which in context means disruption of moral forces. The
captain justifies the criticism of the first morality; for he does,

among all his misdeeds, keep the sixth and ninth commandments. But the kind of evil he commits recalls the doctor of *The Cards of the Gambler* who narrowly escaped death above the jagged mountains and who reflected "the discharged murderer is really afraid that the watchers may read on his face evidence of his compressed diabolic joy in evil done with impunity." [4] The captain, so diabolical that he would hurt himself to hurt others, experiences the same joy as that of a murderous fiend except for a matter of emphasis: he would prefer to let people live and suffer while he watches them squirm under his gaze. The only detraction from his triumph is the implication that John Rodgers, who does not fear him, has possibly already detected the wellspring of his pleasure, evil done with impunity, and therefore scorns him. The captain deliberately visits his evils on his children; but, most significantly, while he fixes his listeners in much the same way that Coleridge's Ancient Mariner held the wedding guest, he never expresses his opinions on parent-children relationships.

Described as a little man clad in boots of elegant leather with something in him "that always watched and crouched," the captain's opinions, the ones which he chooses to express, are always those he knows "with diabolical, uncanny instinct, would offend or hurt his listeners." And he chooses for his listeners the persons in sensitive positions: doctors, priests, solicitors. To them, he would brand the entire island with a chosen vocation "to avoid an honest day's work" and label the priests "our only exportable surplus." His favorite conundrum, one which he poses at moments when anyone would seek to forget the oppressiveness of human existence, is "Is it better to be born and damned than not to be born at all?" The conundrum delights him with its implied hopelessness between "hellfire and dark neance," and he proceeds as if his role of father-devil incarnate is to demonstrate that his children are indeed damned.

In spite of reasonable foreknowledge, Owen Rodgers, visiting Bingen for the first time to witness sheep-dog trials, is not prepared for what he sees below the loft in which he has hidden himself to await the beginning of the show. The captain's voice like a gunshot shouts commands to march and countermarch at his five children rigged in oversized army regalia complete with heavy boots and long rifles. Alfred's clumsy slowness of foot earns him a heavy crack across the ear from the monster who has to stand on tiptoe to reach Alfred's shambling stoop-shouldered height. Looking with curiosity upon the spectacle of his friend's disgrace brings Owen the first feelings of guilt, of being as wicked as the captain. He runs from himself, as well as from the scene of the demon in action, and returns only when summoned.

After the demonstration of the captain's military prowess, Owen next witnesses his superior knowledge of zoology, complete with Latin name, *Melophagus Ovinus,* for the sheep tick and his recital of its life cycle. Likened by Owen to a bad enchanter, Captain Chesney intimidates his listeners, moves like a ruler among sheep and men, and wears his Victoria Cross to remind his audience of his valor against the Boers.[5] Though his whiskers, according to Kinnear, may testify to his virility, an unexpected bald spot on the top of his head seen indoors stabs across Owen's vision as a warning of the captain's morality. Everything about him speaks of deadliness, including a deft movement of his small foot like the fang of the snake on the mantel. He has organized the house like a military establishment with bell-pull summons for the daughters Maeve and Greta, a less personal method than speaking to them; and they function not as people but as solvers of haulage and transport problems. In fact, the captain has reduced all human effort to the economics of supply and demand, including the nightly reading of orders for the next day's work and dismissal of the regiment of five children rather than the customary good night.

For his children, the captain has replaced the so-called formative years with destruction and malice aforethought to teach them their unworthiness. Alfred, with long gangling arms, has earned from schoolmates the nickname "Slobber" for his unavoidable spraying with spittle as he talks. A childhood incident about his identifying a deformed fox terrier as an Austrian dog that was bandy-legged from walking in snow and about his sitting wet-lipped and silent like an Austrian dog himself, unable to reply to his classmates' ridicule, foreshadows his later reaction to abuse of a more serious nature: instead of retaliation, the injury takes another form.

Describing Alfred's falling in love, Kiely writes one of his most lyrical passages, borrowing from an English poet: "He saw her and he knew that he had found the long-awaited, long-expected spring, he knew his heart had found a time to sing, the strength to soar was in his spirit's wing." [6] The laughing, dancing, mouth-organ playing Rose he loves has, to preserve life in her smooth round limbs, found employment as a skivvy, an occupation damned by the captain who, as he requires his children not to do, had married beneath him. When the captain learns from runaway Edmund, whom he strikes in the face before the eyes of mother and brothers and sisters, that Alfred has associated with a skivvy, retribution is swift, painful, and humiliating—even to the mother whom he strikes in the face when she tries to interfere on Alfred's behalf. Alfred, bound naked to a post in the barn, is beaten and left to shiver through the night; and he is told that, if he wants to be like the animals, to live with the animals. His ensuing sexual misdemeanors, after the captain's death, can be traced by sympathizers to the abortion of his first love.

Edmund, brown-haired and somewhat plump with soft, smooth skin, has something of the captain's verbosity as well as his daring, which in Edmund's case is a recklessness that masks cowardice, as is evidenced by his repeated early attempts to run away from home rather than stay and take the abuse. He alone talks in the pained silence that awaits the captain's arrival for nightly orders, just as he talks later to save his skin; he knows from experience the results of the captain's anger, having been, for previous escapades, roped to a post in the byre and beaten with a bog birch-rod until saved by a cottier's interference at risk of life and limb. In spite of almost habitual ill-calculated daring, which usually ends in disaster, he finally succeeds once in reaching the Rodgers home and in obtaining fare to England. After the captain's death, he returns with a beard like his father and with a lavish display of gorgeous clothing.

Francis, destined by his father to supply the quota of one Irish son from each household for the priesthood, grows into a strange, sallow man who is known during Owen's acquaintance with him to have laughed only once—the occasion of Owen's offering to help with the assigned chore of picking up paper left by visitors from the sheep-dog trials—a wild, heinous laugh more like madness than mirth.

Frank's falling into the river after an ill-fated (for him) fishing trip brings on an illness that, almost purposely, demonstrates another skill of the egocentric captain. Owen finds him testing a urine specimen for albumen to diagnose the illness; and Owen, picturing the sweating pallid Frank in agony upstairs while the captain chants descriptions of disabling, dismembering illnesses, is convinced that he can never be a doctor. The medical profession requires detachment from keenly felt bodily ills. From his own horror he insults the captain by inquiring what the doctor had said. From the effects of the illness, when Frank tells of experiences of precognition, he sounds much like his father on creation, necromancy, and damnation; and his unheeded words describe white birds, foretelling death, roosting on the footbridge. As if the air around Bingen House conveys the black art of the magic man Mickey Doran, the captain the following week falls to his death from the footbridge. Having lived by an evil conundrum and having derided Hughie Heron's misunderstanding the word in saying a man had died of a conundrum,[7] the captain dies a death best explained—or was he dead before he fell?—as a conundrum.

The two daughters, Maeve and Greta, have no bodies and no personalities as long as the captain lives. The mother had last appeared in public ten years before at mass in "an old shiny black coat that would disgrace a pauper."

The mystery of the captain's wife, the answer to the question of how anyone could have chosen to marry him, remains to be solved when she regains use of her voice after his death. When Owen first sees her, a shadow come to life, she mesmerizes Owen so that he blurts out his own mother's name in the phrase of sympathy. "He was strict," she says; and she relates the story of a courtship begun when, as a skivvy, she stood in line with the other servants to hear a gramophone play; and of how, when the visiting drunken captain followed her to the kitchen, she struck him with a saucepan. It is a sign of his goodness, she insists, that he did not report her and married her a year later. Too full of care he was, she claims, to bother with a honeymoon; and, to Owen's horror, she stands tottering, lifts a wrinkled face, and sings in a quavering parody of John Rodgers' accomplished performances, the old North Ireland version of the Boer War ballad which parallels her courtship:

> Oh, they marched through the town,
> And their banners were so gay

That I ran quick to the casement
  For to hear the drums play.

Oh, I peeped through the blinds,
  Very cautiously in
Lest the neighbours they might think
  That I was looking at the men.

I heard the drums beat
  And their music was so sweet
But my heart at that moment
  Got a far finer treat,

For the bands' troops were
  The finest I did see
And the captain with the whiskers
  Cast a sly glance at me.

Next we met at a grand ball
  And of course I thought it right
To pretend that we had never met
  Before that same night;

But he knew me at once,
  I could tell by his glance,
And I hung my head and blushed
  When he asked me to dance.

Oh, he stood by my side
  At the end of the set
And the sweet words that he breath-ed
  Oh, I never will forget.

Oh, my heart it is enlisted
  And will never more be free,
Since the captain with the whiskers
  Cast a sly glance at me.

They have marched from the town
  And I never saw them more,
But I often think of Ireland
  And the whiskers that he wore,

And I dream all the night
  And I talk all the day
Of the handsome smiling young man
  Who has gone far away.

> And still I remember
> With superabundant delight
> How we met on the street
> And we danced all the night,
>
> And I keep it in my mind
> How my heart filled with glee
> When the captain with the whiskers
> Cast a sly glance at me.[8]

By Christmas time when Bingen House has for some months been newly decorated in an obvious effort to exorcise the captain's ghost, the mother's fear of him, though she and the rest of the family often vow loyalty to him, returns in the form of visitations. By springtime, she has shrunk to scarcely a wrinkle under the bedclothes, and she confuses visitors with the dead captain. By wet July, she wanders outdoors, delirious, and soon dies with Owen Rodgers rushing with the priest to her bedside. That she could do the captain no harm, Owen thinks, best explains the mystery of that marriage; it corroborates the suspicion that a villain is always in some way a coward.

The kind of evil done with impunity can be only the sort inflicted by the captain on his wife and children; there is no punishment for parents who warp the minds of their children. But with all a son's loyalty, Francis explains, "He was a disappointed man, Owen. I don't know why." Born into a civilian life for which he was not suited and damned to live only one of several possible lives, the captain tried to master several types of proficiency and to impose military regimentation and efficiency on civilian life. Owen, as a medical student in Dublin who tastes the sins of the flesh with an infected prostitute, suffers not pangs of remorse for sin or even unusual physical illness but nightmare visitation from the captain with flickering red eyes asking his eternal conundrum and repeating "I died of a conundrum." In dealing with the inexplicable intangibles of evil, the novel shows that all of life is a conundrum.

III   *The Wake of Reorganization*

From immediate relief to delayed tentative objectivity, but never regret, those who knew the captain move in a series of minor tragedies over a span of years. Thin, hollow-jawed, and pimply-faced Francis, who by nature would have no problem maintaining the dignity of the priesthood, should, because of his training from the captain, have no problem with obedience, celibacy, mortification, or submission of will. When he hands Dr. Grierson the gregarious monsignor's book and occasions a discussion of *coercitio,* he suffers the doctor's banter in silence; but sensitive Owen cannot forgive himself the callousness of reminding Francis of personal experiences with coercion: "For a few awful minutes the captain travelled with us through the deadly sleet." The learned Louvain doctor, talking with Owen in a crowded restaurant catering to the clergy, would not realize that behind his head like a wraith the dead captain leers, "Our only exportable surplus," and echoes his earlier observation of seventeen priests and two nuns on the sidewalk in Dublin between the Nelson Pillar and the Parnell monument.[9] As if the captain had analyzed every human activity, his thoughts intrude in all conversations.

The captain's destruction of Francis comes indirectly through rumors of Maeve's child born out of wedlock. Dr. Grierson reports how a similar experience disillusioned him: "I was a devout neophyte, I was an assiduous student," he explains; but, when he was twenty-six, he realized not his own merit but the respectability of the relatives determines clerical success, and shortly afterward he discovered that a bottle is "the golden road to Samarkand and forgetfulness." So now, with much conjecture about his sister's sin, the Lord Bishops have condescendingly allowed Francis to go forward. A short time later, with Greta nearly dying, he returns in holy stiffness and impotence from Maynooth to beg Owen's help. Although Dr. Grierson names him "the only prop of a falling house," his reliability appears doubtful. Going to Louvain and returning bitter and alcoholic, he has all the signs of becoming another Dr. Grierson. As in Dr. Grierson's despair with Higher Authority, Francis' experience testifies to excessive clerical attention to the forms of religion and not enough to essentials.

Edmund, for his part, disrespectfully returns from England too late for his father's funeral; with permanently waved hair and horn-rimmed spectacles, he is a thriving though repulsive businessman who metaphorically dances on his father's grave through a series of adolescent-type escapades of pure anarchy. As the captain had thought much of death, Edmund wills death, especially by speed. A motorcycle hell-rider, indifferent to all damnation, he causes a brawl and a court case, and finally smashes into a bridge; ironically, he was "never a success at running away." He emerges from a coma of six weeks with a permanently damaged head; the only remnant of his father's management ability is the astuteness required to corral his small son safe from the traffic in a telephone kiosk.

The early dissolution of Bingen House, a wake of anarchy which follows the captain's death, erupts dramatically into a free-for-all brawl with Edmund's blaming the dead captain for Alfred's sexual escapades, Francis' accusing Edmund of mismanaging household affairs, Alfred's accusing Edmund of betraying his secret which lost Rosie for him, and Alfred's finally pulling out Edmund's beard by the roots. Owen, interfering, imagines the captain's ghost darting from the eyes of the snake; outside, he remembers the demons of Michael Doran, now undoubtedly dancing in malevolent joy at the Bingen House chaos.

Though Alfred's perverted desire initiates most of his difficulties, the sins of the father are visited in another form; Alfred would be less liable for lawsuit if the captain had not left him wealthy. With much pride he tells Kinnear, "You see, James, I have the money. Without money you're nobody." Remembering the proud Kruger, the Boer War general who was hanged from a sour apple tree, Owen remembers also the captain's saying, " 'To the Uitlanders in the goldfields, Master Rodgers', Kruger said, 'I have the guns' " (239). Because the captain's zeal for order had occasioned a sergeant to be penalized, the sergeant makes retaliation against the captain's son a personal matter and pursues the case beyond Kinnear's private mediations to settle for money. Not hanged but hounded out of a Dublin slum, Alfred, stone drunk and with false teeth in fragments on the dirty floor, convinces Owen that he is a most fetid Austrian dog and that "everything human rots and rots."

The first indication that life thrives in a swamp, not in clear water, came for Owen through disillusionment with the beautiful Maeve. Having seen her personality emerging as from a shell, given life by the captain's death, Owen first loves her as a delightful, confident, capable woman. Walking with her in proud purity through days of sunlight, he allows the glitter of his ideal to prevent his seeing the truth or doing simple arithmetic. The idyll of her companionship he would not spoil with recognizing the significance of her using Kinnear's tie to hold up her slacks, of her familiarity with the cottier Hughie Heron, of her scarf found in the room formerly occupied by the hotelman Grainger. It ends with Owen's seeing her through binoculars on a hillside, obviously copulating under a raincoat with Molphy, a local boxer. Again, memories of the accuracy of the captain's certainty of evil intrude upon Owen's reflections to confirm his dismay. After this experience, the captain assuredly lives again. There are for Owen no virgins except bronze statues, as if the captain were present to say, "All women, Owen, since they were born at all were born to be damned" (222).

Maeve's unscheduled departure with another man called Beverly turns Owen's thoughts to Greta, who with apparent irrelevance connects Maeve's disgrace with the captain's miserly hoarding of money, but the connection is the sin of wasting any good thing. Owen, loving life and persisting in foolish defiance of the captain, believes it is better to be born and damned than never to be born at all, and he accompanies Greta to bed. But this act of love eventually, though unintentionally, brings about her suicide. It is a taste of love which she cannot keep. Until this experience, the dark polarity of life with or without love remained unknown to her, and she cannot long afterward sustain the stark pain of living without love. For a short time, she can go to the city with Owen and become an excellent manageress of hotel affairs and exhibit the captain's efficiency in solving haulage and transport problems but only until a burst appendix removes her to the hospital, which is no less revolting to Owen the ex-medical student now when he must visit her as a patient. There she rushes to her own despair by insisting she is not loved, obeys impulses to self-destruction, and by her pathos persuades Owen they had not shared love but necromancy. Feeling all her attractiveness lost, he remembers the love ritual as "evil rites on the body of a woman." To end a lonely convalescence, she offers herself to Fee the jockey; and she finally shouts at Owen that he could have escaped the father who twisted the others but he wanted to be afraid. The horror of her predicament turns Owen away temporarily from rediscovered Lucy, but he does not want Greta. After her suicide fall, one of the seventeen priests the captain had counted in one city block arrives to pick up her mangled body as if confirming the captain's jeer at the superfluous clergy.

Maeve, encountered many years later in Dublin, has a seven-year-old son and two black teeth. She speaks of "my son," just as the captain had asserted his ownership with "my son" or "my daughter" rather than by the boy's name. She has forgotten the red setter Gortin Lass, a gift of Owen to her years before, and all the beauties of the past. Far, however, from having received the punishment of the ungodly, she talks about her husband's vacation, like any upright citizen. Her disarming deception, now lost to the role of housewife anxious about her child, is preserved in the faceless son whose character does not register with Owen; he has no ties with the past, no identifiable origins.

Dr. Grierson has accepted gratefully the careful regimentation of a clerical retirement home. Owen learns by letter from Kinnear of Alfred's continued "rummaging under rustic petticoats" and discusses with Macsorley the problems of Ireland and keeps silent within himself the problem of taking a new, city wife whom his children dislike. He imagines the captain's spirit looking upon Alfred and emerging anew in Alfred's illegitimate progeny, upon Edmund sleeping in the sun, and upon Francis praying for the soul of the departed tyrant. Among Dublin's docks and factories, disconcerted by exposure to good and evil and rendered inactive between them, Owen morosely analyzes the parts of his own makeup: from his father, kindness and music; from the learned doctor, burnt-out hopes and whiskey; from the captain, compressed malevolence. Exactly what went wrong with his own life eludes his grasp; but, in recognizing the artificiality of his existence, his failure to be a healer, and his luring visitors to his hotels with artificial decorations and gimmicks, he comes close to realizing what he missed. The realization dawns when he finds Hughie Heron resembling "a great sycamore withering far from its native earth in Magheracolton" while he watches two city fishermen raking up foul weeds not far from where unwanted dogs receive injections to transport them out of this reeking world. Then he recognizes that the beauties of Magheracolton are preserved only in Hughie Heron's song sung in a Dublin pub among city people who never saw Magheracolton. The shift in scene from the natural beauties of Bingen to Dublin's ugliness conveys the theme of reorganization and destruction. Civilization does not re-create the beauties of the past; the necessities of living, for which the farmers left bleak Segully, interfere. At the same time, individuals who remain detached observers are as guilty as the wicked. The captain's attempts to create cosmos out of chaos by imposing harsh discipline only confirm the eternal damnation of the race. His real sin was reorganization, but others have shared the crime in less tangible ways.

Beautiful things, as in beautiful songs, must be consciously preserved against the forces of destruction that are as intangible but yet as real as the captain's personality. Owen's wise, kind father, knowing this fact, had hated the captain who was a reorganizer, a destroyer.

CHAPTER 11

Of Lust and Lore:
Dogs Enjoy the Morning

ART, said Stephen, "is the human disposition of sensible or intelligible matter for an esthetic end." [1] Writing further about esthetic purposes, James Joyce defined three levels of creativity: the lyric, the epic, and the dramatic, of which the famous third level, when the artist refines himself out of existence, has become a favorite of Joyceans. Looking at an individual writer, that third and highest level may be said to be achieved when the accomplished artist in perfect freedom uses the best of all possible techniques and sensible worlds and when, in regard to intelligible matter, he no longer has a proverbial but only an artistic ax to grind.

The difference in artistic levels can be seen by comparing Kiely's early novel, *In a Harbour Green,* with his last, *Dogs Enjoy the Morning.* The artist of the last novel has no need to defend Catholicism, though he writes of a Catholic community with much humor and detachment, or to crusade against either side of any polaric views. Though the setting is much the same in both novels, the communities are different; propriety has given way to freedom of opinion. The Partition between Dublin and North Ireland is now nonexistent; Ireland is now one country of the heart and mind; and, as in *The Captain with the Whiskers,* the characters move freely between their town and Dublin. Point of view also moves between that of the omniscient storyteller and the "I," which is dominant near the end of Part V, through whose mind all has been observed and presented. The story does not end but trickles away with reluctance as the waters pass through the tentaclelike weeds of the old canal; and, certainly, as Kiely asserted in *Modern Irish Fiction,* no story ever ends.[2]

I *A Garden Enclosed*

In *Dogs Enjoy the Morning,* Cosmona, a fair village of the plain, stretches a scant mile between the antique and historic mill at one end and the ruined abbey and hospital at the other. The eighty-year-old miller, Martin Mortell, divides his attention between personally preserving the mill, a structure whose stones provide him an emotional attachment as if they were children, and communally restoring the abbey, built by pious monks of seven centuries before who drained low-lying waters away and called its bit of rising ground the Island of the Living, because, according to legend, bodies buried there did not corrupt; and later it was said that men who prayed there would never die. The abbey, like many similar structures scattered over Ireland, boasts a crumbling stone tower with a circular stairway and encourages taking air and sunshine and scenic views from its open top, one now reinforced with iron railings through efforts of the abbey restoration and preservation committee. The top of the tower, and many are of approximately sixty-five feet in height, can easily become a circular stage for any observers in the area. Climbing to the top of the tower, one sees the salmon river and the winding road from Dublin which passes through Cosmona and turns eastward, crossing an old humpy canal bridge, to the ten-mile-distant village of Crooked Bridge. To the west, the several buildings of an abandoned railway station, in addition to the weed-choked canal, and Cathy Hanafin's fishing hotel where fishermen no longer stop, testify to former flourishing businesses now shifted elsewhere with the advent of the automobile. Cosmona today is a village more frequently passed by than stopped in.

Next to the ruined abbey, religion has turned from monasticism to therapy; the crescent-shaped hospital staffed largely by nuns, with boys and girls carefully segregated in separate wings, ministers to the spiritual needs of convalescents through appropriate prayer rituals and of communicants through religious leaflets disseminated with mixed intentions and results among a singularly unimpressed community. The leaflets, composed by delightfully innocent and devout Sisters Thermometer and Bruno in adoration of the Blessed Virgin, represent the town's best pornographic literature—even though the leaflets must compete with a lurid Solomon and Sheba paperback found incongruously with a Red

Biddy wine bottle on the abbey's chaste and sober steps. The leaflets have superior and gratuitous circulation. Marking an attempt to make the spiritual graphically edifying, they never fail in appreciative, lusty minds to bridge rather than separate the physical and the spiritual: "She is a tree of life to them that lay hold on her; and he that shall retain her is blessed." [3] Such a leaflet, in fact, placed in the hands of an experienced newspaperman jestingly called Lord Laurence Collins, or trenchantly, Lord Muck of Ballymuck, approaches the obscene and the profane at once: "My sister, my spouse, is a garden enclosed, a fountain sealed up. . . . Yea, the Lord of all things hath loved her" (19–20).

The leaflets, placed appropriately on the hotel bar where they should urge propriety and sobriety rather than virility and fertility, receive the mute tribute of the familiar; among decent people, they generally escape comment; but, considering the nuns as the source, even the most brazen scoffer lapses into silence or mirth. The attention of the villagers turns rather to the three living Cawley brothers, their sister Dympna, and her friend Teresa Fallon—five unruly juvenile delinquents famous for unexpected cruelty to and dismemberment of a variety of living things. They and their "home"—called "the Ranch" because of its composition of several scattered and abandoned buses with plywood and cardboard windows—squat at the eastern end of the village on the road to Crooked Bridge. The Cawleys are the weeds of poisonous, identifiable, blatant evil in the garden of Cosmona.

The plot, which spans three days, focuses on a single mating event of the second day and on its sequels that day and the next in the lives of several Cosmona citizens. The clerical student Peter Lane, regaining an unsteady vertical after eighteen months on a spinal frame, the nurse he loves called "the Mouse," the generous doctor and the alluring doctor's wife, the miller, the celibate historian Charles Roe and his sexually frustrated housekeeper, Cousin Grace, picnic on the historic moat from which they view the fornication on the tower of daft Nora and the one-eyed, simple-minded Gabriel Rock. Christy Hanafin, fifteen years absent as a convict, returns briefly and leaves his lonely wife pregnant, thereby unknowingly fulfilling her fondest dreams. The miller's son dies of tropical fevers brought home from sacrificial building of the bridge at the River Kwai, but not before three visiting journalists and a cameraman have obtained his picture and something of his story. Prodigal Teresa Fallon and Dympna Cawley, having brought a thieving Dublin girl home with them, see one brother and the girl hospitalized by a more powerful force, a black man from Liberia; and they depart to establish their police records in another city.

The novel begins with a description of birds flying about the abbey and hospital; the birds are alive and free, but the people are hampered by surgical appliances. Partly, the perfect blending of natural setting and action marks the stylistic advance of this novel over previous novels: "It [the gull] circled above the hospital, then perched, not resting so much as surveying, on the tower as if the grey friars who seven hundred years ago had placed stone on holy stone had been thinking only of the comfort of a bird and of that single moment" (1). This blend of the natural and the màn-made develops a theme which only the very sagacious, perhaps the miller and the priest who dominate the last pages, realize; on this island of the living, each person is closed in his own particular island of the mind; but he thinks he could shock the others who have not his particular brand of knowledge, just as the gull seems to assume monarchy of all he surveys. The perfect harmony of man and nature abides through all human difficulties, preserves the good things of life, and endures.

Stylistically, also, Kiely achieves an accomplished ease in using vernacular dialogue. Relaxing from either seminary or Oxford English, Kiely retains "mad out" instead of "extremely peeved" and such phrases as "It's a wonder all out." Humor is most professional in the dry dialogue of the newspapermen, who have been and done many things, mostly while occupying seats in the local pub. The Kiely predilection for literary allusions blends naturally, also, in the thoughts, for example, of the fatherly miller looking upon three village children, who emerge from his childhood's memory of Longfellow via the sixth reader as "grave Alice and laughing Allegra and Edith with golden hair" (19). There is, also, an artful use of irony. While the newspapermen in the hotel bar speculate on the possibilities of the village whores, a voice from a visiting chest X-ray truck blares via loud-speaker, "You don't have to undress." The names of characters reflect a coy acceptance of human idiosyncrasies: Nurse Walters, called "The Mouse"; Sister Grignon de Montfort called Sister Thermometer; Cousin Grace so designated because she will never be wife or mother; Gabriel, a flying angel on his bicycle; the miller called Martin Mortell while Saint Martin is said to be the patron saint of millers.

Pedantry in folklore and hagiography comes mostly from the village bore, Charles Roe, and only secondarily from Peter Lane, the clerical student drifting further and further from monasticism. Instead of blind reverence for holy men, the residents of the hospital and the community judge them, as well as others, as individuals. No one in this novel is, in the final analysis, a type; but the attempt is to show ideas and persons from several viewpoints. Cousin Grace, for example, covets her beauty title of twenty years earlier; but Charles Roe sees her as the least attractive of all women. Christy Hanafin, returning from bitter exile in prison, views Cosmona as the end of the road and as an example of all life, a "bloody mess." The last of the barges, he says, has been "towed into eternity." An old stone tank now overturned in the grass was once a watering trough for horses. The old stables and passenger waiting room are now ruins. The harbor was once famous for suicides.

The novel includes some thirty characters; it is closely and dramatically unified on the basis of the one common denominator —sex.

II *Somewhat of Lust* [4]

Where a religious leaflet is pronounced a "devout, voluptuous anthology," where history tells that no female was permitted on the Island of the Living, thoughts urged to abstention turn naturally to sex; and *Dogs Enjoy the Morning* provides a variety of approaches to the fond subject before it presents the climactic scene on the top of the phallic tower, a scene which acts as a pivot for altering and generally expanding the views of all. The generous young doctor, content, objective, complacent in his marriage to a wealthy ex-nurse, views the involvement of all in sex with perfect detachment. Routing the voyeur, Gabriel Rock, from his bedroom closet, he can laugh, "I would have left the poor curious divil there, but the wife's fussy" (8), and he conceals the identity of Gabriel as the famous mysterious Peeping Tom who looks at nurses through the lighted hospital windows. His purring, contented wife, however, returns from the picnic trip from which they viewed the tower scene and explodes in anger for the first time; for her, Gabriel's and Nora's escapade has spoiled the feeling of exclusiveness and has exposed as cheap that which had been perfect and private delight.

To Teresa Fallon and Dympna Cawley, two expertly drawn delinquents from families of easy virtue, sex may as well be a family affair, especially when no one is certain whether Enda Cawley is a brother or not; and thievery from the grandparents is honorable because the grandparents have no need of money. Absent without leave from a day's work in the hospital, they view the sights of Dublin with the freedom and superiority of those who have no morals. Caramels provide amusement when placed to adhere to unsuspecting shoes; underclothes newly purchased replace the old which, flushed down public toilets, hopefully will stop the drains. An intoxicated gentleman in a pub mistakes them for ladies and gives them money; Dympna dances with a black man who drunkenly stuffs pound notes into her bra and expresses his joy in "wildcat" leaps,[5] but a new friend, Amantha, robs the black man and runs from him at a roadside inn. The novel is carefully plotted in these details; Dympna has written for the black man the name of Cosmona on a grubby dripmat; Amantha's leaving Dublin to escape his vengeance thereby proves futile.

For the four Cawleys, Teresa, and Amantha, the scene on the tower exposes more opportunity to plague Gabriel Rock, a man of uncertain parentage who derives his last name from a Cawley-hurled missile which deprived him of one eye. With Enda beaten off from persecuting Gabriel by the angry priest, Father Jarlath, they take to their heels and the hills and turn their deviltry on Amantha, unfortunately for her now an acknowledged virgin. Spreadeagled by the three Cawleys and Teresa to teach her the facts of life, Amantha lies helplessly ready for Enda's rape when the black man from Dublin smashes into Enda and makes his way with Amantha. Gabriel's and Nora's lovemaking for a brief time spurs the Cawleys to greater lawlessness, but, shortly, also brings the downfall of their evil dynasty.

Peejay, the hotel handyman, who is five feet four inches of righteousness, defends animals on the basis of their leading purer lives than human beings do. His large white cock, trained to shake hands on command and photographed in action with a hen by the visiting newspapermen, disillusions him, when photographed, more than any people on the tower could. A man of pure and lofty virtue, he sends anonymous tips to the Dublin papers for "the good of the world and the salvation of men's souls." Having lured the Dublin journalists to Cosmona with hint of a delectable Peeping Tom story, he asserts God is a Peeping Tom. The moral implications of his peeping when he opens the envelopes Cousin Grace trusts him to mail from Crooked Bridge, for which she pays what he calls thirty pieces of silver, therefore escape him because of the heights of his moral superiority. With an unfortunate marriage in his past, he regards kissing as filthy, and he devotes his free time to painting garish religious scenes to urge others to piety. He slays the fornicating cock "to redeem the sins of Cosmona."

Cousin Grace, a graying spinster housekeeper who covets her moment of glory of twenty years earlier, ties her long flowing hair back with a red ribbon as in her youth and dyes her underwear red. Having, with her mother's help, earlier rejected all possible suitors as unworthy, she tempts her priestly cousin Charles Roe with lurid postcards of bathing beauties which she tells Peejay, when he mails them, are religious leaflets intended to turn Charles from godless ways; and, for her trouble, she receives in return Charles' and the community's jests at her continence.

Charles Roe, an ex-Jesuit seminarian, wounded in the war, continues in wealthy and idle independence his studies of saints anf folklore; and, according to Cousin Grace, he worships a virginal statue, his Aphrodite, in his garden. Privately regarding Grace as the least alluring of all imaginable and real women, he spurns her attentions as though they come from the devil. Occasionally a paraldehyde needle administered by the doctor calms his passion for jungle heat, a passion carried to the extremity of requiring a tea kettle of boiling water poured into the toilet. Otherwise, in his whiskey-sodden delight, Aphrodite becomes his Eustochium, and he, in pristine purity, a new Saint Jerome and Lord Byron combined. Pornographic religious literature no doubt establishes an unacknowledged link between the two unlikely males that he emulates: "But if those virgins are also virgins, yet because of other faults are not saved by bodily virginity, what will become of those who have prostituted the members of Christ and have turned the temple of the Holy Spirit into a brothel." And he also reads, "Take a millstone and grind meal, strip off thy covering, make bare thy legs, pass over the rivers. Thy nakedness shall be discovered and thy shame shall be seen. . . . She shall sit by the waters of solitude, and putting down her pitcher shall open her feet to every one that passes by" (180–81).

References to the black man's picking his queen, the assaulted Amantha, infuriates Grace with the intentional link to her own moment of glory. "How much better these silly beauty queen competitions would be if the elected queen were publicly deflowered" from Charles Roe sends Grace shivering and sobbing in fury to drown in small bits the last of her lewd postcards and to recognize conclusively out of a storm of emotion the impossibility of marriage with Cousin Charles. Explaining why he left the Jesuits, he says he could not decide whether God is a square or an isosceles triangle. Peter Lane, well on the way to perfect sexual harmony with Nurse Walters, replies confidently, "To goats, he's a goat" (107).

Father Jarlath, an elderly shell-shocked ex-chaplain, once shouted in the midst of hospital quiet "Ego te absolvo" at one of his penitents before he remembered he was not on a battlefield. His sermons of abstention to nuns and nurses, concentrating on the sixth and ninth commandments, provide them a weekly amusement; for they tell among themselves a rumor of his youth when an ex-nun for love of him slashed her throat at the altar rail. Only to the miller on that last peaceful morning does he confide his version of his life's work, with a different intent than they supposed when he preached about the degrading passion of love. The nuns' confessions are scruples, he tells the miller. "And I waste my breath preaching them thundering sermons about the sins of the flesh in the hope it might put something into their heads worth listening to: a real temptation, instead of a scruple about fervour in mental prayer" (248). His final condemnation of his own role comes through his branding Peter Lane as "damn near as bad. A sort of mealy-mouthed Jesuit or a Methodist" (248).

For his part, Peter Lane traverses in three days that gray world of half knowledge to knowledge. Having begun some months earlier in a tickling game with Nurse Walters, he has progressed now to a hand under her skirt behind the protection of a pink screen intended for clerical privacy, and he proceeds to clumsy fornication in the hospital's deserted lavatory. He soon learns to doubt and then to discard priestly injunctions against pollution. A memory of preseminary days when a stranger who wore bicycle clips and had no bicycle, who lifted the skirt of a woman sleeping in a field, and who taunted Peter's ignorance now aids his progress, as do memories of masturbation in a limed outhouse, shaped not unlike a confessional box, where offense of God seemed less likely because God would not choose "to live in the less desirable residential area" (105). Reflecting on Nora and Gabriel on the tower, he resolves that the next time perfect co-ordination will replace clumsiness. To all but Nurse Walters, he remains the bookish prude he was when he entered the hospital eighteen months ealier; but among his conclusions the "I" specu-lates that Peter will realize "there are more altars than that marble altar with its cold linen and candlesticks and flowers" (249).

Cathy Hanafin's story centers about a collection of children's toys in her attic, a collection which represents dreams of unborn children. Having been severely hurt in the past when her husband Christy was sent to jail for stealing from his theater's cashbox, having been hurt also by his other negligences, and having watched his term lengthened for attempted escape, she has bit-terly accepted as impossible any future life together; nor does he, a born wanderer, desire it. When she hides him in her attic and later discovers he has smashed the toys and impaled Little Boy Blue obscenely on the handle of the hotel bar's beer dis-penser, she mutely accepts her fate. Christy, looking from his balcony seat in the attic on the tower performance, comes down from his own tower to seek his indifferent wife, to rifle the till afterward while she sleeps to fulfill the adage of burning his bridges behind him, and to leave Cosmona forever to follow his dreams of fair women to places unknown. Cathy, now, for the first time in her life, has plans to make for the future.

The story essentially belongs to helmeted and goggled Gabriel Rock, whose one desire is to establish a new speed record for his bicycle between Cosmona and Crooked Bridge; but he desires to test man, he says, not the machine. Taunted by the Cawleys to observe the waggle of daft Nora, having peeped at nurses and the doctor's wife, he chases Nora among the tombstones lying "like dominoes"; makes of life and death, as he sought to prove on his bicycle, a game; and possesses her at the top of the tower. His act differs from that of the others only for its commission in daytime, and he makes Peeping Toms of the whole village. Christy finds him, secluded by Cathy in Peejay's hut where Peejay's religious and artistic fanaticism has produced huge murals of village persons representing biblical characters. There shines forth from the walls a gaudy space man or hell's angel, and there sits the original, Gabriel Rock, motionless on a stool; he is the man twice seen by Christy once "mounted on a bicycle and careening through the village, once high on a tower and mounted on the village's female idiot" (204). About to be confined when caught, and confronted by the bitter ex-convict Christy Hanafin, Gabriel protests that he only wanted to break the cycling record to Crooked Bridge. Christy seems to express the attitude of most of the spectators when he replies, "You've broken it too. You got up higher than anyone ever did" (205). Like his angel namesake, who brought word to Mary of her bearing the child Jesus, this cycling hell's angel brings word of life into the daylight of Cosmona.

That dignified "concupiscence of the flesh," as varied as life itself, hereby brought into the open daylight, is made delightful with the cooperation of the pert, laughing Nurse Walters and the smooth piston action of the doctor's wife; made fruitful and comforting for lonely Cathy Hanafin; recognized an impossibility for Cousin Grace and Charles Roe; acknowledged outside his clerical office by Father Jarlath; remembered by the miller; translated into justice by the black man wreaking his vengeance upon the thief Amantha: it transforms foot-stamping Nora into a bliss of memory and continues, no doubt, in numerous hayfields and sidewalk locations where Teresa Fallon and Dympna Cawley ply their timeless trade. As wholesome and as joyful as any "soft-bosomed, sweet-breathing" young women and as natural as climbing the tower for a scenic view, sex unites all people in a commonalty that none can deny.

III *Somewhat of Lore*

The superstitions and folklore of the past of Cosmona, as timeless as the rooks circling the abbey tower, combine with history to unify the past and the present while Peejay, as amateur reporter, and the four professional journalists from Dublin try valiantly to make history of the present. Though characteristically Peejay overlooks the dramatic achievements of the county strong man, Patrick Hoban, who can lie on his back with three men in a wheelbarrow on his incredibly broad chest and practice his deep-breathing exercises, and instead egotistically writes the story of a family squabble between the Hobans and the Cawleys, a grotesque parody both of newspapers and of justice, the village has worthwhile lore. The story and photographs of the one remaining of ten former operative mills have already appeared in the papers, but no newspaper story can record the attachment the miller feels for his handiwork, especially the stones ground to perfection so that they can take the print off an otherwise untouched visiting card for amazed tourists. The machinery, his creation, gives him more independence and a feeling closer to God than could any factory-made machine; and he remembers fondly childhood stories about the mill's devouring the bad boys. To Christy Hanafin, usually bitter and unappreciative, the mill sounds like an orchestra with wheel and river in harmony.

The miller's contentment, however, always vanishes like chaff blown on the wind when he remembers the little that is left of his only son, "like a weed waving in the salmon water." Stephen Mortell's story, as told by Charles Roe, includes a long history of childhood difficulties: of being nicknamed the Dead Man, of going berserk after his marriage, and of shortly thereafter entering the army to escape mill and millstones. Subsequently, he and many other men were ground by the Japanese who, in the end of the war, were themselves ground. Even his father sees little difference in personality between the son as returned veteran and the former morose youth who inherited his melancholy from an alcoholic mother. Meantime, the sight of lily pads reminds the haunted miller of his son's stories of having eaten such pads in the Japanese jungle, just as the pure water of the river reminds him of his son's being kicked into faraway fetid water; snails recall his son's story of eating cooked grass with snails on it; his old tabby reminds him of a man in his son's camp who ate another prisoner's cat raw—skin, guts, claws, all—and was flogged by the other prisoners. The son tells of food thrown to lepers as if they were dogs, of knowing he had diphtheria when polished rice he had eaten came back through his nose, of rampant diseases destroying human bodies from which remnants of living entrails were excreted, of funeral pyres on which bodies dead of typhus danced in the flames, where another type of pagan god, the python, links cruel and fearful humanity with pagan gods of any country's mythological past.

Cosmona's specialist in the past is the garrulous Charles Roe who tells the story of Domnhall the Horse Robber [6] who one day swept a farmer's daughter into his saddle and rode away to his dark cave, never to be seen again. His huge stone chair above the village of Cosmona earns a ritualistic place on Charles Roe's picnic itinerary while the black man of Liberia revives the legend. Also, the miller, silver-haired and white-linen suited, looks like a modern Saint Patrick. With the coming of Christianity, a religious pilgrimage was made barefoot up the mountain,[7] blending with it a pagan festival for the first fruits and the beginning of harvest, when a virgin was chosen to cut the first sheaf; and the girl making the finest bracelets from berries was crowned queen of the harvest. There is a stone pillar [8] with magical qualities; around it a bachelor walking three times at sunrise would acquire success with a maiden.

Charles, having viewed with his party the scene at the top of the tower, remembers other rites of pagan fertility and religious nudity: Lucian of Samosata [9] describes a rite in honor of the goddess Atargatis with a nude male sitting atop a high stone phallus; Heliodorus, spiritual guide of Simeon the Stylite,[10] spent sixty-two of the sixty-five years of his life high in a monastery; holy Serapion [11] walked naked with a nude virgin through the streets of Rome to prove himself indifferent to the desires of the flesh. Charles continues with an account of local fertility rites: maidens dragged their shifts three times through a stream to learn from visions of future husbands whom such might be; and peasants, when the lord of the land had dried the lake around the Island of the Living two centuries before, fed fragments of the dried mud to their cattle to induce fertility. Charles, at home in his garden and muttering that Cousin Grace has driven him to drink, reads about Saint Jerome and Eustochium; [12] walks three times around his Aphrodite; roars at Grace a brief dissertation of Tilly [13] who, with Pappenheim, killed thirty-five thousand people in one night but piously preserved his chastity; and, soused into oblivious sleep, abdicates the prurient affairs of Cosmona's black man to more sober citizens.

Bits of folklore belong to the conversations of others also. Such is the story of Nurse Callaghan who appeared as a ghost to Nurse Walters, a story which the community hopefully prods Nurse Walters to believe. Nurse Callaghan, having died in the nurses' home ten years earlier and having expressed as her dying wish that the boys in their hospital beds be kept well tucked in on cold nights, suggests by the watchful, ghostly continuation of her care a solicitude in which the living find solace. On the matter of pregnancy, there are several helpful bits of folklore: Dympna Cawley believes fervently that the chewing and eating of blotting paper, drinking boiled water that has had rusty nails in it, and the wearing of a miraculous medal about the neck keep her safe from all possible pregnancies. Cathy Hanafin, certain of her pregnancy, remembers tinker and Gypsy methods of determining the sex of an unborn child: the tinker women scattered oats on a plate and knew by the way the oats fell whether the child would be boy or girl, and the Gypsy woman broke an egg in a bowl and drowned it in spit; the next morning she knew, if yolk and white were mixed, she would bear a daughter; if separated, a son. Country women, to become pregnant, hoped a bullock might lick them or a cricket from the hearth alight on them or that wild geese or ducks would fly in a prescribed pattern.

Cathy Hanafin's brothers are called Shadow and Substance by reason of folklore about the arrival of twins; their characters were predetermined by the order of their births. James Tarrant, called Substance, is dominant because he came second out of the womb, thereby pushing John, or Shadow before him. James is stout and solid, his brother thin, stooped, prematurely gray, all of which the folklore of Cosmona could have foretold; in the order of conception James was first, planted securely farthest in, and would always be lucky. Shadow is panting and peevish and occupies by nature a subordinate position. Because of another bit of folklore, Cathy casts the destroyed Little Boy Blue's body to the waves; water, a universal symbol of eternity, would preserve friendship and affection where fire would destroy it.

Christy Hanafin—inspired by brandy in the strange surroundings of Peejay's painted hut with the murdered white cock on the floor before him and for audience a dejected Gabriel about to be condemned to the black hole for his private deeds done in public—begins telling his own story of a black hole. Prison was a place where time, unmeasured, was eternity; where dreams were nightmares of unfulfilled desire; where personal belongings could not be secreted in the rectum because that too was unceremoniously examined with flashlight; where revenge for any insult was retaliated by a kidney beating from guard and warder;

where the governor was god; and where fear of dying in prison drives a man to attempt escape and adds years to an almost completed sentence. So powerfully does Christy relive those horrors that he frightens Gabriel into running away in the darkness just as he, Christy, will run forever.

Peter Lane's particular brand of lore—that of the saints—comes from his year in a Jesuit seminary. "Noli me tangere," Jesus had said to a holy woman; and Peter, at first enjoying the attentions of Nurse Walters, considers the sin of breaking the "ne tangus" rule and of developing inordinate affection.[14] A short time later, he wonders whether the pillar Saint Simeon the Stylite sat on was not a phallic pillar rather than a spiritual one. And very early he remembers a passage from the Canticle of Canticles which, thinking of Nurse Walters, he will ask Sister Thermometer to include in her next leaflet. It describes queens, concubines, and young maidens, of which one is perfect, the chosen one of her mother. Of this passage he finds that Saint Francis of Sezze [15] has offered explanation: all those lovely women are really saints and saintly souls of lesser perfections. As far as Peter is concerned, the One perfect Virgin comes carrying bottles and bedpans.

With thoughts turning more and more to the secular, Peter Lane permits his saints to abdicate in favor of a lustier but wholesome story, the story of Treasure Island, his nickname for his own pink-screened monastic hospital cell; there he has discovered his treasure, the nurse. His reading of the Revelation of Saint John the Divine after his attempted fornication with Nurse Walters leaves him little more edified, for Balaam's teaching of Balac to commit fornication seems harmless enough in his present unrepentant state. Saint Charles of Sezze [16] threatened to fill the devil's mouth with dung, but Peter Lane desires no such vengeance. The visiting brothers who seek to edify him [17] with thoughts of Saint Thomas Aquinas likewise fail to convince. For, in the end, nearly all his thoughts turn to the attractions of the flesh. Sister Thermometer's leaflet applies particularly to Nurse Walters: "Take hold on her and she shall exalt thee. Thou shalt be glorified by her when thou shalt embrace her. . . . She will strengthen him, and make a straight way to him, and give him joy, and will disclose her secrets to him" (256).

Somewhat as *The Cards of the Gambler* unified the past and

present through pagan and Christian symbols, so *Dogs Enjoy the Morning* blends the pagan, the Christian, the present, the past, the lore of saints and of sex. For example, did the mills stop on Saint Martin's Day in honor of the patron saint or because, before the saints, the people thought the harvest god died when the grain was ground? The black man sat only by coincidence, perhaps, like a second Dark Domnhall, on the slope of Cosmona to capture his woman. The gentle Father Jarlath, Cousin Grace says with much disgust, walks like Finn MacCool [18] with three hounds at his heels. Peejay grew a beard after the disruption of his marriage because Jesus had a beard "and since the time of Jesus he was the man most crucified." The once sacrosanct abbey tower became a living phallic symbol; the miller's only son died as God's only son died to save the lives of others. The mill wheel turns as the earth turns. One of the visiting journalists declares that the life of nature is "demonstrably superior to the ordered life of reason because the river flowed free and the canal was mostly choked with weeds" (150). Meanwhile, the atrociously immoral Enda Cawley plays music that cheers a youth doomed to live his few remaining years without rising from a hospital spinal frame. Peter Lane observes that man kneels to pray and to make love. The black man, looming out of an unknown Liberian past, knew only eight or nine words in English, but his often-repeated phrase, "Cosmona, one, two, three," finally concluded with "much fuck," declares not only his purpose in coming to Cosmona but also, indeed, the purpose of most of Cosmona's citizens.

In the end, the miller whose son has died and the priest who walks like Finn MacCool and shares, evidently, Finn's views on lustiness, greet a new day after that historic day of drama in peaceful Cosmona. "The extent to which dogs enjoy the morning," Father Jarlath declares, "is one of the few things that have kept him believing in the existence and goodness of God" (244), that and man's ability to fly—a combination, in dogs and flying, of instinct and of reason. Like the man-made canal and the natural river, the pagan and the Christian, continence and prurience, the past and the present, the why of continued existence is bounded by such polarities. These dichotomies explain the implications of both beginning and end in the last paragraph, "More and more harvest fields are every day being opened for the reaper," as well as why the story does not end but closes with a reaffirmation of faith in the future. Like the religious leaflets binding the physical and the spiritual, the "Harvest fields are happy-hunting-grounds for foraging birds."

CHAPTER 12

"An Image of the Irish Writer"

IN the totality of Kiely's fictional works, the cast of characters includes several whose occupations he has personal knowledge of: the writer, the doctor, the hospital patient, the literary connoisseur, the Jesuit priest. The writers as characters include two amateurs who profit from the freedom of expression: Bernard Fiddis of *In a Harbour Green,* who confides to his diary what he cannot say in public; and Jim MacKenna of *There Was an Ancient House,* who writes poems as a guilty diversion from the rigors of the Jesuit novitiate. But by far the largest group of writers are the professionals, such as George Butler of *Honey Seems Bitter* who is a drama critic. Also, Brother Barragry *(Ancient House),* Brian Flood *(Call for a Miracle),* and the four visitors to Cosmona *(Dogs Enjoy the Morning)* are journalists who ply their trade with a remarkable thoroughness in spite of much time spent in pubs. A sketch of Kiely himself in this role gleams through the character of Lord Laurence Collins *(Dogs);* he typically makes bad rhymes ("aquaduct" with "fucked"), quotes numerous minor authors, and carries in his pocket a notebook of delectable facts to fill his conversation, such as a title of a book, "Raped on the Railway, or, a True Story of a Lady who was first Ravished and then Flagellated on the Scotch Express" *(Dogs, 242).* To explain their mission in Cosmona, the journalists exchange witticisms about their editor's newsworthy preference for human suffering; the editor "prefers people laid low by polio or twisted by terrible cancers. He says the public loves them. He loves them. Holes in the heart, madam, are too cheerful. They preclude resurrection" *(Dogs, 134).* But in spite of their wry humor, the omniscient narrator, who enters in the first person to oversee the closing fourteen pages of the novel, pays tribute to the professionalism of the four journalists: "Knowing them, they will, I know, try to tell the story as colourfully and accurately as they can" *(Dogs, 244).*

The penchant for quotations, as seen in some of the journalists, often doubles as a favorite trait of the priests and thereby recalls Kiely's statement that he once considered the priesthood as a means to scholarship. The clerical scholars who quote from learned and obscure tomes include Peter Quinn *(Land Without Stars)*, Jim MacKenna *(Ancient House)*, Dr. Grierson *(Captain)*, and Peter Lane and Charles Roe *(Dogs)*. Other than Laurence Collins *(Dogs)*, the book lover, when coupled with journalism as a trade, best appears in the character of Brian Flood *(Miracle)*; and, when coupled with illness, in the character of Donagh Hartigan *(Honey Seems Bitter)*.

Illness most frequently takes the form of the lumbar or tubercular spine which Kiely personally experienced, especially for Dave Murray *(Miracle)*, Jim MacKenna *(Ancient House)*, and Peter Lane *(Dogs)*. The illness may be terminal (Dave Murray) or recuperative (Jim MacKenna, Peter Lane) but Donagh Hartigan of *Honey Seems Bitter* is the only character recovering from illness who is allowed the fear and the danger of self-pity. The illness usually requires approximately eighteen months of immobility and leads to a change of heart or an altered viewpoint. A clerical student visiting Peter Lane sums up the experience: "when the famous Dean Stanley came to his deathbed he said to somebody: Things seem so different when one assumes the horizontal" *(Dogs,* 29).

The doctors who attend the patients are always somewhat philosophers. The gambling doctor of *Cards of a Gambler* challenges Death as life's greatest gamble; and the doctor of *Dogs,* who is untried as yet by the rigors of economic or physical discomfort, has a generous sympathy for both mental and physical aberration. Owen Rodgers *(Captain)* begins a medical career with his views sensitized by his father, John Rodgers, who has a rare gift for music and song combined with a love of nature and a sense of humor; at the same time, the son's views are distorted by association with the diabolical Captain. Owen, somewhat like the priests who abandon their careers, philosophizes too much and necessarily abandons his medical training in favor of a simplified life as a hotel manager.

Kiely's priests as characters always have freedom of thought and expression, so that the reader eventually sees them first as persons and second as clerics. Except for Father Peter *(Miracle)*, whom

Kiely gives a sympathetic and somewhat idealized character as a successful priest, and Dr. Grierson *(Captain)*, the clerics generally enter a novitiate and withdraw before ordination. Often they cannot reconcile scholarship with dogma because their search for ultimate truth exposes too many kinds of truth, as in the example of Dr. Grierson, who frets against his superior's ("Higher Authority's") failure to appreciate folk values; and Charles Roe *(Dogs)*, who stated he left the clergy because "I could never make up my mind whether God was a square or an isosceles triangle" *(Dogs*, 107). This statement reveals his love for, and extensive knowledge of, mythology and folklore; the square and triangle, ancient symbols commonly represented in the four points of the cross and the Holy Trinity, had a validity long preceding and supplementing Christianity. Father Peter, who succeeds, and the other characters who abandon the priesthood as a vocation (such as Peter Quinn of *Land Without Stars*, Jim MacKenna of *Ancient House*, and Peter Lane of *Dogs*), are able to direct their doubts and their knowledge into positive acceptance of all learning and experience: hence comes Peter's answer that "To goats he's [God] a goat." Father Jarlath of *Dogs* is an interesting study of a balance between priestly office and private speculation; as a shell-shocked ex-chaplain, at times he has periods of lucidity which lead the reader to suspect his mind is clearer than he pretends.

Nationalism for the identity of a character was indeed "written out" in Kiely's early work through the characters of Davy Quinn *(Land Without Stars)* and Bernard Fiddis *(Harbour)*, though the intensity of the particular trait is much reduced in the latter book. For a more recent view of Kiely's attitude toward nationalism, one may consult his article "Ulster After the Bludgeons" in *The Nation* (May 19, 1969). In this article he cites civil rights marches as a new element in the contention between Unionists and Nationalists and lays the blame for the present difficulties on the conservatives who must "keep alive the ancient politico-sectarian hatreds." [1] These hatreds are fed by the oratory of the Reverend Ian Paisley and his followers who "hold that all civil rights marchers, who are in protest against electoral abuses and sectarian and/or political discrimination in the giving of housing and employment, are, in reality, Romanists or Communists, or rebels against Queen and country, or members of the Irish Republican

[159]

Army, or Fenians, or the bleeding, perishing lot all rolled into one." [2]

Kiely offers no simple solution for North Ireland's problems; and his own fiction, for which he frequently draws backgrounds and characters from disparate regions to unite them in a Northern fictional setting, may be said to have metaphorically bridged the political gap. There is, also, a deep abhorrence of violence reflected in Kiely's conversation and in his literary characters. At the same time, although at least two of his novels have dominant atmospheres of evil, the evil is not political. In *The Cards of the Gambler,* evil is the knowledge of imminent death, which is personified in a little man who carries a black bag; and Kiely evokes an atmosphere of foreboding by combining animated environment with personal emotion: "Thunder pranced on the roof until the building shook. Bright lightning came and went. The downpour and the wind wrestled in the street. The red curtains came bellying into the room and ill-fastened shutters swung crashing open . . . the figure crouched in a corner of the iron balcony outside the window. An ape? A bat? a cunning little man with a black bag? Darkness and bright lightning and again darkness, and fingers or claws tearing at his throat, his half-strangled voice crying out in agony" (*Cards,* 162). In *Captain,* which one reader said resembles the work of Ambrose Bierce,[3] Kiely evokes an atmosphere of desperate horror from the personality of the Captain and his effects on persons and surroundings: "Warily I circled his living foot. It darted like the fang of a snake excised from the monster on the marble mantelpiece. The marble was as cold as they say a corpse is, when my left palm rested on it. The grate looked as cold as if it had never known a fire" (*Captain,* 31). *Dogs* also has passages of horror, but these are relieved by more frequent passages of humor and by the varieties of personalities in the town of Cosmona. Horror is generally limited to the dying son of the miller—his illness and his memories: "The sweaty forehead was too big for the shrunken body. Dry lips babbled of horrors that came streaming from the jungle of the brain. The water of the rivers was vicious with leeches and crocodiles. Diseases grew with the rank grass. Bodies, almost skeletons, squatted in rows excreting into boreholes the remnants of their entrails" (*Dogs,* 120).

Always the tone of the writing is quiet, controlled; and the atmosphere, whatever its type—be it horror or humor—seems to evolve from understatement, almost from indirection: "With academic detachment Lord Laurence, who knew a lot about buildings, surveyed the baronial hall of Charles Roe and pronounced it fine, nineteenth-century, canal-company gothic" (*Dogs,* 150). Or the humor may be expressed in a phrase so brief that it nearly escapes notice: a hangover, for example, is parenthetically defined as "the Irish time lag." [4] The dominant quality of style is the natural rhythms of Irish speech: "But there was a quare strain in Jenny Orr's family. She had a brother was put away in the end for religious mania" (*Dogs,* 218). Reflecting on the bawdy humor, the human sorrow, the beauty of nature—all of which make up *Dogs Enjoy the Morning*—with vividness of description and originality in imagery, one reader commented, "The writing is gorgeous." [5]

Kiely's view of the Irish writer in general is expressed in his essay "The Whores on the Half-Doors or An Image of the Irish Writer." He deplores the current status of the Irish writer, asking, "Who wants in his own country or anywhere else to be regarded as a cut between the village idiot and a tinker who might steal the chickens, or a market-stroller who might steal cherries from maidens or wives from husbands?" [6] He discusses the writer's need for foreign markets, primarily London and New York, because the population of Ireland is small, and cites this factor as responsible for some of the distrust among his countrymen. The strongest factor, however, is the fear that the writer will show some of his countrymen as less than ideal. He concludes that the Irish writer today, "helped by that safety valve of publication in London and New York," has the freedom to write as he pleases, seeking accurate self-expression of his people and his environment; and he lists twenty-one contemporary Irish authors who do so. "The moles," [7] he writes, "are in a minority, and Ireland is Ireland" still.

Notes and References

Preface

1. *Counties of Contention, A Study of the Origins and Implications of the Partition of Ireland* (Cork, 1945).
2. Letter to the author, March 31, 1966.
3. "Ulster After the Bludgeons," *The Nation*, CCVIII (May 19, 1969), 628–31.
4. "The Whores on the Half-Doors or An Image of the Irish Writer," *Conor Cruise O'Brien Introduces Ireland*, ed. Owen Dudley Edwards (New York, 1969), p. 158.
5. The early writing appeared chiefly in the *Irish Bookman* and in *The Capuchin Annual*.

Chapter One

1. See Chapter 4, *In a Harbour Green* (London, 1949). This title abbreviated *Harbour*.
2. *The Captain with the Whiskers* (New York, 1961), p. 159. Hereafter abbreviated *Captain*.
3. See *A Journey to the Seven Streams* (London, 1963), pp. 189–206. Hereafter abbreviated *Journey*.
4. For a discussion of this novel, see Chapter 5.
5. This and succeeding verbal comments are from a taped interview, May 29–31, 1967. Hereafter referred to as *Tape*.
6. "Long After O'Neill," *The Capuchin Annual*, XIII (1943), 244.
7. *Ibid.*, p. 240.
8. The Omagh poet was Andy McLaughlin, whom Kiely describes in the essay "The Whores on the Half-Doors."
9. For background in Irish heroes, refer to Seumas MacManus, *The Story of the Irish Race* (New York, 1944).
10. Described in *Harbour*.
11. See the short story, "A Cow in the House," *Texas Quarterly*, IV (Winter, 1963), 39–49.

12. *Poor Scholar: A Study of William Carleton (1794–1869)* (London, 1947), p. 9. Hereafter referred to as *Poor Scholar*.

13. Emo Paric (Emo Park) is described in *There Was an Ancient House*.

14. See *Dogs Enjoy the Morning*, especially the relationship of Nurse Walters and Peter Lane, for development of this topic.

15. Letter to the author, dated October 25, 1969.

16. *Poor Scholar*, p. 4.

17. William Carleton, *Parra Sastha: or the History of Paddy-Go-Easy and His Wife Nancy* (Dublin, 1845).

18. *Harbour*, p. 205.

19. "In the heart of Old New England," *The Irish Times*, (October 4, 1966), or see William Butler Yeats, "In Memory of Major Robert Gregory."

20. Thomas F. Staley, "Notes and Comments," *James Joyce Quarterly*, VIII (Fall, 1970), 1–2. See Kiely's article, "The Artist on the Giant's Grave," *A Bash in the Tunnel*, ed. John Ryan (London, 1970), pp. 235–41.

21. *Tape*.

22. In a letter to the author dated October 25, 1967, Kiely wrote, "The earliest material Senan used (some dreadful poems) were in a quarterly (now defunct) called "Bonaventura." There were other things in other magazines (even lesser ones) but I've forgotten them —which would be the kindest thing to do with them."

23. John McCormack (1884–1945), an operatic and concert tenor; Jack Butler Yeats (1871–1957), Irish landscape and genre painter and brother of the poet William Butler Yeats; Maud Gonne MacBride (1866–1953), a famous beauty and revolutionist, beloved of William Butler Yeats.

24. "Enter Mr. Chesterton," *Catholic Mind*, XLIII (August, 1945), 497–503, and *Irish Ecclesiastical Record*, LXV (January, 1945), 28–34.

25. Of Francis MacManus, Kiely wrote in a letter to the author dated February 23, 1967, "I had read and admired him when I was in secondary school and from the first moment I met him he was guide, counselor, and friend until he died last year—i.e. November, 1965." See also "In Memoriam: Francis MacManus 1909–1966," *The Kilkenny Magazine*, XIV (Spring/Summer, 1966), 121–36.

26. The incident is reported by Norma Lugar, "Obituary Started It All, Claims Noted Irish Author," *The Roanoke Times* (April 22, 1965), 14.

27. *Ibid.*

28. *Tape*.

Chapter Two

1. The Act of Partition was signed by Irish delegates in London on December 6, 1921, and ratified by the Dail Eireann in Dublin on January 7, 1922.

2. "Man from the Pampas," *The Capuchin Annual,* XVIII (1948), p. 433.

3. "The House at Derrynane," *The. Capuchin Annual,* XVI (November, 1946), 393–407.

4. "Poor Scholar," *Irish Bookman,* I (August, 1946), 20–33.

5. *Poor Scholar,* p. 154. Hereafter page numbers in parentheses after the quotation.

6. David J. O'Donoghue, *The Life of William Carleton,* 2 vols. (London, 1896).

7. Maria Edgeworth (1767–1849) wrote *Castle Rackrent;* see *Poor Scholar,* pp. 115–17. For Charles Lever and Thomas Davis, see *Poor Scholar,* pp. 130–32. Charles Lever (1806–72) wrote *Harry Lorrequer,* and *Charles O'Malley.* Thomas Davis (1814–45) was a Young Ireland leader and founder of the *Nation* newspaper. Daniel O'Connell (1775–1847), the celebrated Liberator of Irish Catholics; see *Poor Scholar,* p. 177.

8. Gerald Griffin (1803–40), playwright and novelist of Limerick, Ireland, wrote *The Collegians* and *The Colleen Bawn.* John Banim (1798–1842), a novelist and dramatist of Kilkenny, co-authored *O'Hara Tales* with his brother Michael.

9. *Counties of Contention,* p. 17.

10. The phrase appears in Yeats's poem "The Rose Tree."

11. A review by James A. MacCauley, in *Irish Historical Studies,* V (March, 1946), 105–7, disputed several points in *Counties of Contention.*

12. All these essays appeared in the *Irish Bookman.*

13. *Modern Irish Fiction* (Dublin, 1950), p. 3.

14. The height of irony regarding censorship came with the banning of Kiely's *There Was an Ancient House,* a novel about his year in Jesuit seminary.

15. Theodore Dreiser wrote, according to Kiely, "at the urging of his brother" Indiana's song, "On the Banks of the Wabash." See Kiely, "On the Road to Chicago and the Great Lakes," *The Irish Times* (April 20, 1967), 10.

16. Thomas Altizer, of "God is dead" fame, an acquaintance of Kiely's first year at Emory.

17. Refer also to John Horgan and Sean MacReamoinn, "Report on the Churches," *Eire-Ireland,* I (Winter, 1966), 83–86.

18. "Joe the Post: or a Portrait of the Irishman as a Mole," *Northwest Review,* IX (Fall/Winter 1967–68), 110.

19. "Ripeness Was Not All: John Barth's *Giles Goat-Boy,*" *The Hollins Critic,* III (December, 1966), 1–12.

20. This essay in typescript.

Chapter Three

1. Sean McMahon, "The Black North," *Eire-Ireland,* I (Summer, 1966), 69.

2. *Journey,* p. 35. Hereafter page numbers in parentheses.

3. *Captain,* p. 33.

4. "The King's Shilling," *Irish Bookman,* I (August, 1947), 33–77.

5. "Soldier, Red Soldier," *The Kilkenny Magazine,* IX (Spring, 1963), 7–22, and *Journey,* pp. 189–206.

6. "Rich and Rare Were the Gems She Wore," *Irish Writing,* XV (June, 1951), 5–16, and *Journey,* pp. 119–36.

7. "A Great God's Angel Standing," *New Yorker,* XLIV (August 24, 1968), 28–34.

8. "The Bright Graves," in *Journey,* pp. 207–21.

9. "Ten Pretty Girls," in *Journey,* pp. 32–48.

10. "The Enchanted Palace," in *Journey,* pp. 108–18.

11. "A Ball of Malt and Madame Butterfly," *Kenyon Review,* XXXI (2, 1969), 215–36.

12. "Heroes in the Dark House," *New Yorker,* XXIV (January 17, 1959), 28–32, and in *Journey,* pp. 19–31.

13. "Blackbird on the Bramble Bough," *Irish Bookman,* I (September, 1946), 41–51, and in *Journey,* pp. 151–62.

14. "Mon Ami, Emile," *The Kilkenny Magazine,* IV (Summer, 1961), 13–23, and in *Journey,* pp. 177–88.

15. "The Little Wrens and Robins," *New Yorker,* XLVI (April 4, 1970), 49–58.

16. "The Little Bishop" in manuscript.

17. "Wild Rover No More," *Northwest Review,* VIII (Spring, 1967), 52–64.

18. "The Dogs in the Great Glen," *New Yorker,* XXXVI (October 8, 1960), 42–48, and in *Journey,* pp. 222–38.

19. "A Walk in the Wheat," published in *The Lamp,* a New York magazine of short duration, which I have not been able to trace; this comment prepared from Kiely's typescript.

20. "The Weavers at the Mill," *The Kilkenny Magazine,* XI (Spring/Summer, 1964), 8–25. The lifeboat exploits of the old man, Eamon, in this story was an actual experience of the Rosslear lifeboat men rescuing the crew of a broken tanker in Holyhead and was a newspaper assignment which Kiely covered.

21. *Ibid.*, p. 25.

22. "The White Wild Bronco," *New Yorker*, XXXIV (December 20, 1958), 24–26, and in *Journey*, pp. 11–18.

23. "A View from the Treetop," *New Yorker*, XXXVII (August 26, 1961), 24–32, and in *Journey*, pp. 49–70. Kiely wrote in a letter to the author dated January 5, 1968, "The village described is Duleek, County Louth, but certain features are borrowed from the battlefield of Aughrim in Galway, part of the famous Battle of the Boyne in July, 1690. The schoolmaster who ran the museum was Martin Joyce of Aughrim. The old schoolmaster was Martin Brennan of Duleek, then retired, now deceased. The original of the inspector was Inspector Dale, who visited the schools in the North" when Kiely was a boy.

24. "The Pilgrims," *Irish Writing*, X (January, 1950), 47–56, and in *Journey*, pp. 71–86.

25. "The House in Jail Square," *New Yorker*, XXXVIII (December 8, 1962), 50–58, and in *Journey*, 87–107. Also in *Threshold*, XXI (Summer, 1967), 137–57.

26. "The Wild Boy," *New Yorker*, XXXV (January 30, 1960), 29–33, and in *Journey*, pp. 137–50.

27. "Homes on the Mountain," in *Journey*, pp. 163–76, appeared under title "Houses on the Mountain," *New Yorker*, XXXV (December 26, 1959), 24–28.

28. "The Shortest Way Home," *New Yorker*, XXXVIII (March 17, 1962), 38–45, and in *Journey*, pp. 239–63.

29. "A Bottle of Brown Sherry," *Kenyon Review*, XXVI (Spring, 1964), 317–31.

30. "A Cow in the House," *Texas Quarterly*, IV (Winter, 1963), 39–49.

31. "A Journey to the Seven Streams," *New Yorker*, XXXVII (May 6, 1961), 42–48, and in *Journey*, pp. 264–85.

Chapter Four

1. Egan O'Rahilly, or Aodhagan O Rathaille (c. 1670–1728) is one of Kerry's most celebrated Gaelic poets. A statue of him by sculptor Seamus Murphy may be seen on College Street in Killarney. Kiely's article, "Land Without Stars," in *The Capuchin Annual*, XV (November, 1945), 206–22, describes Kiely's search for O'Rahilly memorabilia in Kerry and Cork and combines travelogue and literary comment.

2. McMahon, *Eire-Ireland*, p. 69.

3. Again, this Jesuit seminary is described in *There Was an Ancient House*. See Chapter 9.

4. Kiely reports there was also a locked room full of such statues in the manor house during his seminary year there.

5. *Land Without Stars* (London, 1946), p. 4. Hereafter page numbers in parentheses.

6. Padraic Pearse, August 1, 1915, funeral oration for Jeremiah O'Donovan Rossa, a hero of the Fenian rising of 1867: "They [Britain] have left us our Fenian dead, and while Ireland holds these graves, Ireland unfree shall never be at peace." See *The Irish Uprising, 1916–1922* (New York, 1966), p. 24.

Chapter Five

1. "A Present from Donegal," *The Capuchin Annual*, XV (1944), 186

2. *Harbour*, p. 68. Hereafter page numbers in parentheses.

3. For comment on propriety as a part of Omagh's town life, see Chapter 1.

4. Northern Ireland typically would vote Unionist at this time; the term means union of North Ireland with Great Britain.

5. These realistic details come from observation of Omagh as a garrison town.

6. For additional discussion of Kiely's view of children, see Part V, Chapter III.

7. These are the nostalgic details of the home town, described in Chapter 1, which makes this Kiely's favorite novel.

8. Cf. Mrs. Kavanagh of *Honey Seems Bitter*, pp. 88–96.

9. See note on "Paddy-Go-Easy" in Chapter 1.

10. *Dogs Enjoy the Morning*, discussed in Chapter 11 this text, contains the ultimate development of this theme.

Chapter Six

1. The spinal ailment is an autobiographic detail which is adapted also to *There Was an Ancient House* and *Dogs Enjoy the Morning*.

2. Dublin's General Post Office was the scene of the 1916 Easter Week Rebellion.

3. *Call for a Miracle* (London, 1950), p. 287. Hereafter page numbers in parentheses. Abbreviated *Miracle*.

4. See, for example, Yeats's poem, "A Prayer for My Daughter," which ends, "Ceremony's a name for the rich horn/ And custom for the spreading laurel tree."

5. See Kiely's biography of William Carleton, discussed in Chapter 2 this text.

6. Richard Harrity book review in *New York Herald Tribune Book Review*, (July 22, 1951), 6.

7. Contrasted with Mrs. McCarthy's necessity to relax "from piosity into uncharity," such a sympathetic portrayal of a clergyman empha-

sizes Kiely's aversion to insincerity in religion and controverts the concept of his rebellion against religion.

8. Doran Hurley was a United States free-lance journalist who wrote for *The Capuchin Annual* and *The Father Matthew Record.* His review, a clipping in Kiely's possession, is from an unascertained Catholic periodical.

9. Richard Harrity, "Dublin Varieties of This Thing Called Love," *New York Herald Tribune Book Review* (July 22, 1951), 6.

10. James Kelly, "The Quietly Sad Irishmen," *The Times Book Review* (July 22, 1951), 4.

11. Nash K. Burger, "Books of The Times," *New York Times* (July 23, 1951).

12. Kevin Sullivan, "Questing Hearts," *America* (August 11, 1951), 462.

13. Bernardine Kielty, "Books to Know About," *Book of the Month Magazine,* clipping undated.

Chapter Seven

1. *Honey Seems Bitter* (London, 1954), p. 61. Hereafter page numbers in parentheses after the quotations. Abbreviated *Honey.*

2. The "fairy hill," or earth mound, described is at Navan Fort in the Boyne River Valley, also described by Sir William Wilde, father of Oscar Wilde, in *Beauties of the Boyne and Black Water.*

3. Letter to the author, January 5, 1968.

4. Review signed P. P., "A Nasty Novel," *Irish Independent* (February 27, 1952).

5. See review by Ann F. Wolfe, "Round Robin's Murder," *Saturday Review of Literature* (October 18, 1952), 19–20.

6. Another accusation of the *Irish Independent* review previously cited.

7. Marcus Aurelius, *Meditations* (New York, 1945), p. 67.

Chapter Eight

1. *Honey,* p. 116.

2. *The Cards of the Gambler,* (London, 1953), p. 4. Hereafter page numbers in parentheses. Abbreviated *Cards.*

3. Harold Bayley, *The Lost Language of Symbolism,* II (New York, 1951), p. 187.

4. An excellent source for this type information is Philip Wheelwright, *The Burning Fountain, A Study in the Language of Symbolism* (Bloomington, 1954).

5. Refer to J. E. Circlot, *A Dictionary of Symbols* (New York, 1962) p. 223.

6. *Ibid.,* p. 248.

7. See William Butler Yeats, *A Vision.*

8. T. S. Eliot, *The Complete Poems and Plays, 1909–1950* (New York, 1952), p. 145.

9. Refer to George Ferguson, *Signs and Symbols in Christian Art* (New York, 1961), p. 113.

10. Sir James Frazer, *The Golden Bough* (New York, 1949), p. 713.

Chapter Nine

1. *There Was an Ancient House* (London, 1955), p. 1. Hereafter page numbers in parentheses. Abbreviated *Ancient House.*

2. Kiely wrote in a letter to the author dated January 24, 1968:

The setting of "Ancient House" is Emo Park, County Laois (once Queen's County). It is still the Jesuit Novitiate. The title is now (I think) extinct. The Countess (Aline was her name) of Portarlington became a Catholic and is buried in the parish church in Emo village.

The place is to the west of the Dublin-Cork road, between Monasterevan (where John Count McCormack lived) and Portlaoise (once called Maryborough). The nearby town of Portarlington has marked traces of the French Huguenots, even to the old-French style houses—back to front so to speak, i.e. backs to the street, fronts looking inwards to old walled gardens. Between Emo Crossroads and Portlaoise is Maryborough Heath and to the East of it the Rock of Dunamase or Dunamace.

3. "Religious" means monastic and as in the phrase "the true religious" is a noun.

4. British publications accept quotation of poetry in paragraph form. Quotation from p. 110 of *Ancient House.*

5. For a Kiely version of how religion gives way to speculation about other matters in a hospital, see *Dogs Enjoy the Morning.*

6. Relapse into the vernacular changes *e* sounds to *a* as in "Jesus" ("Jasus"), "decent" ("dacent"), "easy" ("aisy").

7. Kiely's observations of the loneliness of the parish priest, sometimes the only thoroughly educated man in a remote area, is founded in sympathetic personal opinion. See also Chapter 10 this text for comment on Dr. Grierson of *Captain.*

8. See also *Dogs,* Chapter 11 this text.

9. A lay brother affiliates with a religious order but has not taken vows of priesthood.

10. A type of fish.

11. Kiely here indulges word play on Brinsley MacNamara's novel *The Valley of the Squinting Windows.*

Chapter Ten

1. *Captain,* p. 283. Hereafter page numbers in parentheses.
2. Kiely stated that he had this novel in mind but no house for its setting (he was "genuinely house hunting") when Peter Grant in the the town of Clonmaney in County Donegal asked that Kiely cover the sheep-dog trials for the newspaper because Kiely had earlier written a story about the Glenguard fishermen. There in Clonmaney he found the house built against the headland with the river running around it and wrote it into his novel as Bingen House and included also the sheep-dog trials that he had witnessed (*Tape*).
3. *Gambler,* p. 80.
4. *Ibid.,* p. 145.
5. Kiely here makes use of his father's tales of Boer War exploits.
6. The English poet is Maurice Baring, a friend of Chesterton and Hilaire Belloc. Quoted from *Captain,* p. 41.
7. The conundrum began as a joke with Kiely's friends Judge Jonathan Donlevy, Seamus Murphy the sculptor, and Eamon Crawley who said he knew a man who died of a conundrum.
8. This North Ireland version of the ballad is from a tape recording of Kiely's singing it—reproduced faithfully because not easily available otherwise in American print.
9. Kiely here reports a personal experience from counting the clergy while riding down Dublin's O'Connell street in a bus.

Chapter Eleven

1. James Joyce, *A Portrait of the Artist as a Young Man* (New York, 1966), p. 207.
2. See Chapter 2 this text.
3. *Dogs Enjoy the Morning* (London, 1968), p. 8. Page numbers hereafter in parentheses. Abbreviated *Dogs.*
4. The subtitle for this section and the next comes from the novel's epigraph, "I wolde go the middel weie/ And write a boke between the tweie,/ Somewhat of lust, somewhat of lore," from the *Confessio Amantis* of John Gower. Kiely at one time had planned to make the last line of the epigraph the title of the book.
5. Kiely's description of a man's executing a "wildcat" leap, or somersault in midair, comes from personal observation.
6. Domnhall of Ireland was King of Tara and had his royal seat in County Donegal in the seventh century.
7. The most famous of such pilgrimages, still conducted annually on the last Sunday in July, is that at Croagh Patrick, near Westport, County Mayo, Ireland's Holy Mountain where Saint Patrick is said to have fasted for forty days.

8. One of many monoliths found throughout Ireland from prehistoric times.

9. Kiely's background from Jesuit days and the reading of the lives of the saints is here evident, as in *There Was an Ancient House*.

10. Simeon Stylites the Younger of the sixth century lived on a pillar uninterruptedly for sixty-nine years.

11. Serapion was a second century Bishop of Antioch praised by Saint Jerome.

12. Eustochium officially collated manuscripts for Saint Jerome's translation of the Bible and directed a nunnery at Bethlehem.

13. Johan Tserclaes Tilly (1559–1632) was a Flemish field marshal. The atrocities at Magdeburg (1631) are attributed to his men.

14. See Chapter 9 for "ne tangus" rule and for injunctions against inordinate affection, both requirements of Jesuit training.

15. Francis of Sezze, an assistant of Saint Charles of Sezze.

16. Saint Charles of Sezze died in 1670. Of his many mystic experiences, it was said that a ray of light from the Sacred Host pierced his heart.

17. Also described in Chapter 9, a rule of the Jesuit Order required conversation be directed, usually to the examples of the saints, for edification. The resulting stultification and irrelevance provide humor.

18. Finn MacCool, a legendary giant and hero, lived in the third century and had a residence in Kildare.

Chapter Twelve

1. "Ulster After the Bludgeons," 630.

2. *Ibid.*

3. Ambrose Bierce (1842–1914). His best known gruesome story is "Incident at Owl Creek Bridge."

4. "The Whores on the Half-Doors," p. 153.

5. Letter to Kiely from Perry Kusweton, agent, November 7, 1967, quoting a reader for Atlantic Monthly Press.

6. "The Whores on the Half-Doors," p. 152.

7. For the description of moles as an Irish type, see Kiely's article "Joe the Post: or a Portrait of the Irishman as a Mole," and see Chapter 2 this work. Kiely applies the term especially to Joseph Holloway, who kept a journal of the Abbey Theatre.

Selected Bibliography

PRIMARY SOURCES

1. Novels

Call for a Miracle. London, Jonathan Cape, 1950. Also New York: E. P. Dutton, 1951.

The Captain with the Whiskers. London: Methuen, 1960. Also New York: Criterion Books, 1961.

The Cards of the Gambler. London: Methuen, 1953.

Dogs Enjoy the Morning. London: Victor Gollancz, 1968.

Honey Seems Bitter; London: Methuen, 1952. Also, New York: E. P. Dutton, 1952.

In a Harbour Green. London: Jonathan Cape, 1949. Also, New York: E. P. Dutton, 1950.

Land Without Stars. London: Christopher Johnson, 1946.

There Was an Ancient House. London: Methuen, 1955.

2. Short Fiction

"A Ball of Malt and Madame Butterfly," *Kenyon Review*, XXXI (2, 1969), 215–36.

"Blackbird on a Bramble Bough," *Irish Bookman*, I (September, 1946), 41–51, and in *Journey*, pp. 151–62.

"A Bottle of Brown Sherry," *Kenyon Review*, XXVI (Spring, 1964), 317–31.

"The Bright Graves," *Journey*, pp. 207–221.

"A Cow in the House," *Texas Quarterly*, IV (Winter, 1963), 39–49.

"The Dogs in the Great Glen," *New Yorker*, XXXVI (October 8, 1960) 42–48, and *Journey*, pp. 222–38.

"Excerpt from *The Captain with the Whiskers*," *Irish Writing*, XXXVI (Autumn/Winter, 1956–57), 131–43.

"A Great God's Angel Standing," *New Yorker*, XLIV (August 24, 1968), 28–34.

"Heroes in the Dark House," *New Yorker*, XXXIV (January 17, 1959), 28–32, and *Journey*, pp. 19–31.

"The House in Jail Square," *New Yorker*, XXXVIII (December 8, 1962), 50–58, and *Journey*, pp. 87–107. Also in *Threshold*, XXI (Summer, 1967), 137–57.

"Houses on the Mountain," *New Yorker*, XXXV (December 26, 1959), 24–28, and *Journey*, pp. 163–76.

"A Journey to the Seven Streams," *New Yorker*, XXXVII (May 6, 1961), 42–48, and *Journey*, pp. 264–85.

"The King's Shilling," *Irish Bookman*, I (August, 1947), 33–77.

"The Little Wrens and Robins, *New Yorker*, XLVI (April 4, 1970), 49–58.

"Mon Ami, Emile," *The Kilkenny Magazine*, IV (Summer, 1961), 13–23, and *Journey*, pp. 177–88.

"Pilgrims," *Irish Writing*, X (January, 1950), 47–56, and *Journey*, pp. 71–86.

"Rich and Rare Were the Gems She Wore," *Irish Writing*, XV (June, 1951), 5–16, and *Journey*, pp. 119–36.

"The Rock," *The Bell*, XIX (July, 1954), 17–23. This excerpt is from *There Was an Ancient House*.

"The Shortest Way Home," *New Yorker*, XXXVIII (March 17, 1962), 38–45, and *Journey*, pp. 239–63.

"Soldier, Red Soldier," *The Kilkenny Magazine*, IX (Spring, 1963), 7–22, and *Journey*, pp. 189–206.

"Steady Boys and Step Together," *Irish Writing*, XXVI (March, 1954), 36–49.

"The Top of the Tower: Two Fragments from a Novel," *Shenandoah*, IV (Summer, 1965), 79–95. An excerpt from *Dogs*.

"A View from the Treetop," *New Yorker*, XXXVII (August 26, 1961), 24–32, and *Journey*, pp. 49–70.

"The Weavers at the Mill," *The Kilkenny Magazine*, XI (Spring/Summer, 1964), 8–25.

"The White Wild Bronco," *New Yorker*, XXXIV (December 20, 1958), 24–26, and *Journey*, pp. 11–18.

"The Wild Boy," *New Yorker*, XXXV (January 30, 1960), 29–33, and *Journey*, pp. 137–50.

"Wild Rover No More," *Northwest Review*, VIII (Spring, 1967), 52–64.

3. *Short Story Collection*

A Journey to the Seven Streams: Seventeen Stories. London: Methuen, 1962.

4. *Nonfiction: Essays, Reviews, Criticism*

"The American Movement and William Saroyan," *Irish Ecclesiastical Record*, LX (February, 1947), 101–12.

"The Artist on the Giant's Grave," *A Bash in the Tunnel*, ed. John Ryan. London: Clifton Books, 1970. (About James Joyce).

Selected Bibliography

"Bundoran," *Ireland of the Welcomes,* IV (July/August, 1955), 4–7.
"Canon Sheehan: The Reluctant Novelist," *Irish Writing,* XXXVII (Autumn, 1957), 35–45.
"Chronicle by Rushlight," *Irish Bookman,* II (January, 1948), 23–35. (Criticism of Daniel Corkery).
"Clay and Gods and Men," *Irish Bookman,* I (October, 1946), 9–21. (Criticism of James Stephens).
"Comment on Carlyle," *Irish Ecclesiastical Record,* LXVII (April, 1946), 223–31.
"Connachtman's Grumbles," *Irish Bookman,* I (January, 1947), 27–39. (Criticism of Liam O'Flaherty).
"Core of Colum's Ireland," *Irish Monthly,* LXXVII (October, 1949), 448–52.
Counties of Contention: A Study of the Origins and Implications of the Partition of Ireland. Cork, Ireland: Mercier Press, 1945.
"Dublin Letter," *America,* LXXXIII (November 25, 1950), 492; LXXXIV (August 12, 1951), 230; LXXXIV (March 17, 1951), 700; LXXXVII (July 12, 1952), 381–82; LXCII (October 2, 1954), 16–17; LXCIV (March 17, 1956), 665.
"Elizabeth Bowen," *Irish Monthly,* LXXVIII (April, 1950), 175–81. (An excerpt from *Modern Irish Fiction*)
"Enter Mr. Chesterton," *Catholic Mind,* XLIII (August, 1945), 497–503; also in *Irish Ecclesiastical Record,* LXV (January, 1945), 28–34.
"The Feast of Lughnasa," *The Kilkenny Magazine,* X (Autumn/Winter, 1963), 59–64.
"Fun After Death," *The New York Times Book Review* (November 12, 1967), 1, 75. (Review of Flann O'Brien, *The Third Policeman*)
"The Giant's Causeway," *Ireland of the Welcomes,* XV (July/August, 1966), 6–9.
"The Great Gazebo," *Eire-Ireland,* II (Winter, 1967), 72–86.
"The House at Darrynane," *The Capuchin Annual,* XVI (November, 1946), 393–407. (History of Daniel O'Connell)
"In Memoriam: Francis MacManus, 1909–1966," *The Kilkenny Magazine,* XIV (Spring/Summer, 1966), 121–36.
"Ireland," *Kenyon Review,* XXXI (4, 1968), 463–69.
Irish miscellany, in *The Irish Times* fortnightly, 1968 to the present.
"The Island in the Heart," *The Irish Times* (March 7, 1967). (Criticism of George Moore)
"Joe the Post: or a Portrait of the Irishman as a Mole," *Northwest Review,* IX (Fall/Winter 1967–1968), 110–16. Also in *The Kilkenny Magazine,* XVI–XVII (Spring, 1969), 64–72.

"Journey in Ulster," *The Capuchin Annual*, XIII (1943), 495–501.
(Signed Conal Casey)

"A Key to James Joyce," *Irish Bookman*, II (December, 1947), 9–19.
(Criticism of *A Skeleton Key to Finnegans Wake* by Joseph
Campbell and Henry Morton Robinson)

"Land Without Stars," *The Capuchin Annual*, XV (1945), 206–22.
(Criticism of Egan O'Rahilly)

"Letter from Ireland," *Books on Trial*, XIV (November, 1955), 128.

"Letters from America," in *The Irish Times* fortnightly, September,
1964 to Summer, 1968.

"Liam O'Flaherty: a Story of Discontent," *Month*, II (new series)
(September, 1949), 183–93.

"Long After O'Neill," *The Capuchin Annual*, XIII (1943), 239–50.

"Man from the Pampas," *The Capuchin Annual*, XVIII (1948), 428–
36. (Criticism of William Bulfin)

"Marooned Modernist?" *Irish Bookman*, II (July, 1948), 59–70.
(Criticism of Sean O Faolain)

Modern Irish Fiction. Dublin: Golden Eagle Books, 1950.

"Orange Lily," *Irish Bookman*, I (June, 1947), 11–25. (Criticism of
Shan F. Bullock)

"Otway's Magic Mountain," *The Bell*, XV (January, 1948), 53–60.
(Criticism of Caesar Otway)

"Poor Scholar," *Irish Bookman*, I (August, 1946), 20–33. (Criticism
and biography of William Carleton)

*Poor Scholar, A Study of the Works and Days of William Carleton
(1794–1869)*. New York and London: Sheed and Ward, 1948.

"Praise God for Ireland," *Irish Monthly*, LXXVI (September, 1948),
402–6.

"A Present from Donegal," *The Capuchin Annual*, XII (1944), 186–92.

"Ripeness Was Not All: John Barth's *Giles Goat-Boy*," *The Hollins
Critic*, III (December, 1966), 1–12.

"Scene in Passing," *Ireland of the Welcomes*, XV (May/June, 1966),
21–27.

" 'So Grand on . . . ,' " *Irish Bookman*, I (November, 1946), 17–30.
(Criticism of Francis Sylvester Mahony, known as Father Prout)

"The Tale of the Tailor," *The Kilkenny Magazine*, XII/XIII (Spring,
1965), 29–34. (Also a radio broadcast)

"A Terrible Beauty," *The Irish Uprising, 1916–1922*. New York: The
Macmillan Company, 1966.

"Thanksgiving in the Hoosegow," *Nation*, CCVII (November 25,
1968), 553–57.

"That Old Triangle: a Memory of Brendan Behan," *The Hollins Critic*,
II (February, 1965), 1–12.

Selected Bibliography

"'. . . To Seek the Truth,'" *Irish Bookman,* II (December, 1946) 75–78. (Review of *Towards a University* by David Kennedy)

"Ulster after the Bludgeons," *Nation,* CCVIII (May 19, 1969), 628–31.

"Uncrowned King," *The New York Times Book Review* (July 10, 1966), 6, 22. (Review of *The Parnell Tragedy* by Jules Abels)

"Unpredictable Dynamics," *Irish Writing,* XII (September, 1950), 65–66. (Review of *The Withered Branch: Six Studies in the Modern Novel* by D. S. Savage)

"The Whores on the Half-Doors," *Conor Cruise O'Brien Introduces Ireland,* ed. Owen Dudley Edwards. New York: McGraw Hill, 1970, pp. 148–61.

"Yesterday is Forever," *Irish Bookman,* I (April/May, 1947), 11–26. (Criticism of Jane Barlow)

5. *Unpublished Manuscripts*

"The Jeweller's Boy," story, broadcast over Radio Eireann, Dublin.

"The Little Bishop," story.

SECONDARY SOURCES

1. For criticism of Kiely's work, only one article, in addition to my own, and one biographical sketch in a book are available. Several personality sketches have appeared, however, in newspapers. The book reviews quoted in the text appear in footnotes to the text and are not repeated here.

BARRETT, F. BOYD. "Benedict Kiely, 1919–." *Catholic Authors,* II. Matthew Hoehn, ed. Newark, New Jersey: Saint Mary's Abbey, 1952. Brief biographical sketch with books published through 1951 included in comment.

ECKLEY, GRACE. "The Fiction of Benedict Kiely," *Eire-Ireland,* III (Winter, 1968), 55–65. Includes comment on all twelve books of Kiely's plus some short stories.

MACREAMOINN, SEAN. "Markings," *RTE Guide* (January 13, 1967), 9. This personality sketch has merit based on personal acquaintance with Kiely, though the author erroneously states that Kiely learned Gaelic at Rosses Point, County Sligo. The place was the Rosses of Donegal.

MCMAHON, SEAN. "Books and Authors: The Black North," *Eire-Ireland,* I (Summer, 1966), 63–73. Also, entitled "The Black North" in *Threshold,* XXI (Summer, 1967), 158–174. Compares Kiely with two other fiction writers of Northern Ireland, Michael McLaverty and Brian Moore.

2. Supplementary Sources Cited in This Work

BAYLEY, HAROLD. *The Lost Language of Symbolism*. 2 volumes. New York: Barnes and Noble, 1951. Especially applicable to the symbols in *Cards of the Gambler,* this book is a basic text on symbols.

BENEDICTINE MONKS. *The Book of the Saints*. New York: The Macmillan Company, 1947. A basic and simplified text to identify the many saints mentioned in Kiely's works.

CIRLOT, J. E. *A Dictionary of Symbols*. New York: Philosophical Library, 1962. A scholarly, condensed, and somewhat advanced reference work on symbols.

FERGUSON, GEORGE. *Signs and Symbols in Christian Art*. New York: Oxford University Press, 1961. A basic text for use with *Cards of the Gambler.*

HOAGLAND, KATHLEEN, ed, *1000 Years of Irish Poetry*. New York: Grosset and Dunlap, 1962. A good collection containing several poems quoted by Kiely, including Padraic Pearse's "The Fool" from which Kiely took the title *Call for a Miracle.*

KILLANIN, LORD, and MICHAEL V. DUIGNAN. *The Shell Guide to Ireland*. Second edition. London: Ebury Press and George Rainbird; New York: Norton, 1967. The most comprehensive book available for places, dates, personalities of Ireland.

MACMANUS, SEUMAS. *The Story of the Irish Race*. New York: The Devin-Adair Company, 1944. A somewhat impassioned but accurate source for historical backgrounds.

WHEELWRIGHT, PHILIP. *The Burning Fountain*. Bloomington, Indiana: University Press, 1954. A basic study of universal symbols and folklore.

Index

Index

Index